WE'RE NO ANGELS

Copyright © 1990 by David Mamet

Published by Grove Weidenfeld
A division of Wheatland Corporation
841 Broadway
New York, NY 10003-4793

Published in Canada by General Publishing Company, Ltd.

Library of Congress Cataloging-in-Publication Data

Mamet, David.
We're no angels: a screenplay/written by David Mamet. — 1st ed.
p.   cm.
ISBN 0-8021-3202-2 (alk. paper)
I. Title.
PN1997.W445   1990

791.43'72—dc20   89-25804
                                                              CIP

Manufactured in the United States of America

Printed on acid-free paper

Designed by Irving Perkins Associates

First Edition 1990

1   3   5   7   9   10   8   6   4   2

We're No Angels

A Screenplay Written by

DAVID MAMET

GROVE WEIDENFELD
New York

The author wishes to thank Bella Spewack
and the Estate of Albert Husson for their
cooperation in the publication of his
screenplay for *We're No Angels*.

THE CAST

NED/"FATHER RILEY"	Robert De Niro
JIM/"FATHER BROWN"	Sean Penn
MOLLY	Demi Moore
FATHER LEVESQUE	Hoyt Axton
DEPUTY	Bruno Kirby
THE WARDEN	Ray McAnally
BOBBY	James Russo
THE TRANSLATOR	Wallace Shawn
THE SHERIFF	Jay Brazeau
MRS. BLAIR	Elizabeth Lawrence
YOUNG MONK	John Reilly
BISHOP NOGULICH	Ken Buhay
LITTLE GIRL	Jessica Jickels

THE CREDITS

Produced by	Art Linson
Directed by	Neil Jordan
Written by	David Mamet
Director of Photography	Philippe Rousselot
Production Designer	Wolf Kroeger
Coproducer	Fred Caruso
Executive Producer	Robert De Niro
Costume Designer	Theoni V. Aldredge
Editor	Joke Van Wijk
Supervising Editor	Mick Audsley
Composer	George Fenton

We're No Angels

1935. A penitentiary, near the Canadian border.

1 *Exterior: Prison—Night.*
   Drifting snow. The camera cranes past a barbed-wire fence, past the penitentiary sign, past pacing guards with dogs on walkways, to reveal the prison beyond, searchlights flaring around it.

2 *Interior: Prison—Night.*
   A mine, built into the mountainside, in which the prisoners are working. Camera reveals the various levels of the mine, a blur of steam, smoke, spurting gas jets, the prisoners, covered in dust, working like moles against the rock face. Guards with dogs pace on the walkways above.

3 *Angle: Two convicts,* NED *and* JIM, *covered in fine dust, working a large vat.*

4 *Angle: Tannoy speakers fixed to the walkways. The guards pacing. A siren sounds, and the prisoners cease work, begin to shuffle down to the bottom level.*

The WARDEN, *a heavyset man with a riding crop, emerges through a cloud of steam onto the main walkway.*

WARDEN: The taking of a life is no minor matter. (*Beat.*) Nor do we do it lightly. (*Beat.*) This man has killed, and he *will* be killed.

5   *Angle: The* WARDEN, *from below, over the heads of the prisoners, pacing above them.*

WARDEN: Take him out. This is the end of crime, gentlemen. And it is called "punishment."

Two guards drag out a chained convict (BOBBY).

WARDEN: This man will be taken down, his head shaved; he will receive confession if he wishes it. We will then test the apparatus; the lights will dim, once, twice, the *third* time; then his soul will be in that New Place. I leave you to conjecture where that place will be.

BOBBY *being walked down the line of convicts, the CAMERA MOVES with him.*

WARDEN: I want no demonstrations. I want no *comments,* I have no doubts but your thoughts will be troubled. Keep them to yourselves.

As he passes two convicts, NED *and* JIM:

BOB: So long, guys . . .

JIM (*sotto*): So long, Bobby.

GUARD: No talking.

JIM (*sotto*): Hey, whaddya going to *do* to him: take away his *commissary* . . . ? Son of a bitch . . .

The CAMERA STAYS on NED *and* JIM.

NED (*sotto*): Keep it down, Jim.

JIM (*sotto*): Son of a bitch . . .

WARDEN (*voice-over*): And there you have it, gentlemen. I wish you a good evening.

BOB *being walked down the spiral staircase. The* WARDEN *speaks to his assistant.*

WARDEN: . . . Lock 'em up. . . .

The cell doors are opened; the convicts retire into their cells.

6   *Interior: Ned and Jim's cell.*

7   *Angle: A "pretty girl" pinup.*

JIM (*voice-over*): Can you believe it, can you believe it, Neddy . . . ?

8   *Angle:* NED, *on his bunk, looks at the pinup.* JIM, *on the lower bunk, smokes a cigarette.*

NED: I can believe most anything. My problem is I just don't care.

JIM: They're taking Bobby to the bakery.

NED: Sometimes it *happens* that way.

JIM: . . . that the guy's gonna *die*, and that's it . . . ?

NED: Hey, what the fuck, he's a murderer . . . what's your question . . . ?

JIM: That, that's the end of it? That, that he goes in that room . . .

NED: . . . and he goes in that room and they light him up and that's the end of it and there's no eternal life for his soul and the cruelty of the world . . . izzat the thing? Izzat your problem this fine evening . . . ?

JIM: Yes . . .

NED: You wanna talk to the chaplain.

JIM: Well, I'm talking to you. . . .

NED: I'm busy. I've got my mind on higher things.

JIM: I feel bad, Ned.

NED: Do your own time.

NED *pulls down the pinup girl poster and looks at it. A* GUARD *appears at the cell door.*

GUARD: *You* two . . .

He starts opening the door. NED *and* JIM *look at each other confusedly. The* GUARD *throws in a length of chain.*

GUARD: . . . put these on.

9 *Interior: Prison Corridor—Night.*

NED *and* JIM, *manacled together, are marched down the corridor, the* GUARD *behind them.*

JIM: Just tell me what it *is*, just tell me what it *is*. . . .

The GUARD *raps* JIM *in the kidneys with the stick.*

GUARD: Keep walking. . . .

NED *looks at* JIM.

10   Interior: Electrocution Complex—Night.

The electric chair; a guard fussing over it.

11   Angle: JIM *and* NED *are walked into the anteroom by the* GUARD, *look at the electric chair. The* GUARD *pushes them down on the bench.*

GUARD: The warden said, any man on the floor tonight gets chained, now shut it up, you hear me . . . ?

As NED *and* JIM *sit in the anteroom, the guard in the electric chair room makes a motion, and the lights dim, go out for a moment, then come back on.*

NED (*sotto to* JIM): Life is a hellhole, pally.

BOB *is walked through the anteroom by two guards. He is attended by a* PRIEST. *He nods at* JIM *and* NED. *He is walked across the anteroom. A door is opened. We see him seated, and a barber throws a cloth over him and starts shaving his head. He looks over at* NED *and* JIM. *They look on, terrified.*

The door to the barber room is closed. The WARDEN *comes INTO THE PICTURE.* NED *and* JIM *rise.*

WARDEN: You two were talking. (*Beat.*) Answer me, you two were talking during my speech.

JIM: I . . .

The WARDEN *swipes at his face with his riding crop.*

WARDEN: You *swine* . . . you *swine* . . . (*To his guards.*) Hold him down. . . .

Two guards hold down NED; *two others turn* JIM *with his back to the* WARDEN, *rip* JIM's *shirt off his back.*

12   *Angle:* JIM, *his face to the* CAMERA, *the* WARDEN *behind him, whipping him savagely.*

WARDEN: You *swine*, you want order? *I'll* give you order: *I'll* give you order! You want a *lesson* . . . ? Is that what you want . . . !

A GUARD *comes up to the* WARDEN.

GUARD: Warden, they're ready. . . .

The WARDEN *stops, turns to the* GUARD, *motions at the electric chair, where there is a doctor and several guards standing by.*

GUARD: They're ready, sir. . . .

The WARDEN *lowers his riding crop.*

WARDEN (*to one of the guards*): Keep them here, we'll beat the other one afterwards.

The WARDEN *turns, walks, followed by the other guards, into the execution chamber. He closes the door after him.*

13   *Angle:* NED *and* JIM *alone on the bench, one guard standing beyond them.* JIM *sobs;* NED *tries to comfort him.*

NED: It's all right, it's all right, Jimmy. . . .

JIM: Oh, Ned, I'm in bad shape. . . .

PRIEST (*voice-over*): And the Lord shall judge His people and repent Himself for His servants, when He seeth that their power is gone. . . .

NED *lifts up his head.*

14   *Angle:* BOB, *his head now shaved, being walked out of the barber room, accompanied by the* PRIEST *and two guards.* BOB *stops beside* NED *and* JIM. *He looks ahead, transfixed.*

PRIEST: And there is none shut up or left, and He shall say where are their gods, their rock, in whom they trusted . . . ?

NED *hangs his head. The lights dim, flicker, and go out. (Beat.) Several* SHOTS *ring out. The lights come back on.* BOB *is standing, holding a gun on a guard. His two guards are dead on the floor.* BOB *runs to the door of the execution chamber and throws a massive bolt, preventing those beyond from entering.*

PRIEST: Don't do this, my son. . . .

BOB: Shut the hell up.

He hits the PRIEST *on the side of the head with his gun. The* PRIEST *falls.* BOB *looks around, takes the doctors' smocks off a hook on the wall, and throws them to* NED *and* JIM.

BOB: Here, put these on.

15   *Interior: Prison Corridor—Night.*

Two doctors, seen from the back, pushing BOB *on a trolley down the corridor. Guards rushing past them TOWARD THE CAMERA.*

One guard turns to look at the doctors.

NED (*back to* CAMERA): We're taking him to the infirmary. . . .

The guard nods, rushes on.

15A   Angle: The legs of the doctors manacled together.

15B   Angle: BOB *on the trolley,* NED *and* JIM, *one in the doctor's shirt and collar and the other in his coat.* BOB *holds the revolver.*

NED: I'm not sure this is such a good idea.

BOB: I didn't ask you, Neddy.

NED: Bob, they catch us now, they'll kill us.

BOB: Welcome aboard.

The group comes to a walkway above the mine complex, a huge stairway falling downward. The siren begins to ring. BOB *leaps out of the trolley. Guards are running up the stairs toward them.* BOB *shoots one.* NED *and* JIM *are horrified, look at* BOB.

BOB: That's right; we're all in it now!

He shoves the trolley down the stairs toward the other guards, running up.

15C   Angle: The base of the stairs, guards falling backward under the impact of the trolley. The convicts escaping upward, way above.

15D   Angle: Upper levels of mine. BOB *running down a corridor,* NED *and* JIM *behind him. He comes to a corner, where a large boiler is steaming. A guard rounds the corner, and* BOB *pulls the boiler plug, encasing him in steam.*

16   Point of View: The guard, screaming, flailing in the steam.

16A   Angle: Guards, seen through the gridded walkway at their feet, running, shooting up.

16B   *Angle:* BOBBY, *shooting through the grids. He drags* NED *and* JIM *on.*

BOB: We going or we dying?

16C   *Angle: Upper levels of mine. The convicts running from the flying bullets.* BOB *pulls open a metal door, and we see the snowstorm raging outside against the face of the mountain and a bottomless drop.*

NED: Bob . . .

BOB: You ever heard the phrase "nothing to lose . . ."?

He pushes them out, then jumps himself.

17   *Exterior: Mine—Night.*

NED *and* JIM, *chained together, fall in deep snow.* BOBBY *falls beside them.* BOB *rises, runs into the storm.* NED *tries to drag* JIM *up.*

JIM: Oh, my God . . . oh, my God . . .

Searchlights pop on from the towers above them. NED *drags* JIMMY *through the snow to the base of the towers. They tumble down the slope, out of shot.*

18   *Exterior: Base of Prison—Night.*

NED *and* JIM *tumble and slide down the mountainside. They burrow through the snow, underneath the barbed-wire fence. They run into the storm, as all the lights in the prison come on behind them.*

19   *Angle: Door of kennels. Dogs pouring out, snarling, charging, running to the hole in the fence, dragging guards with them.*

19A   *Angle: Outside the fence. Dogs howling, the* WARDEN *and guards blundering helplessly through the snowstorm.*

20   *Exterior: Snowy Woods Bridge—Day.*

Angle: A doe, seen on the bridge. Doe moves; we PAN with the doe, PAST a bundle on the ground under the bridge. Doe moves OUT OF THE FRAME; PULL IN on the bundle, which is NED *and* JIM, *huddled together, shivering.*

NED: Wake up. (*Pause.*) Jim. Wake up.

JIM *wakes up.*

They get up.

NED: Come on. Come on, down across the river and we're free.

JIM: I'm cold.

NED: Baby, I'm cold, too. Come on. Come on. Walk it out.

JIM: I'm cold.

They start to walk.

21   *Angle: Their feet, chained together.*

JIM: What happened to Bobby, do you think?

NED: Uh-huh.

JIM: Do you think they got 'im, Neddy?

NED: Look at this. . . .

22   *Exterior: Snow-covered Road—Day.*

Stopped at the snow-covered road, looking at a poster. A picture of the Weeping Virgin, and a huge arrow, and the legend TWO MILES.

23   *Angle Insert: The poster.*

"*Patronize the local Brandon merchants. When in Brandon visit the famous Shrine of St. Ann, the Weeping Virgin.*"

"*Do not neglect to show hospitality to strangers, for thereby some have entertained angels unawares.*" *Hebrews 13:1.*

24   *Angle: The two reading the sign.* NED *turns away.* JIM *reads.*

JIM (*reads*): "Do not neglect to show hospitality to strangers, for thereby some have entertained angels unawares. Hebrews thirteen: one."

NED: Very touching . . .

JIM: Hebrews . . .

NED: Wait a second . . . !

NED *becomes very alert. Listens. Sound Effect: An old car approaching.*

NED: Get down!

JIM, *roused from his reverie on the sign and the Scripture, looks dreamily around.* NED *pulls him down.*

25   *Angle: The two of them crouched down in the snow.* NED *looks up.*

26   *Point of View Angle: An old car coming down the road.*

27   *Angle:* NED *looking; something else catches his eyes.*

28   *Point of View Angle: The same road, but now the doe we saw previously has wandered out into the road.*

29   *Angle:* NED *and* JIM *both looking.*

30   *Angle: The car. The* OLD WOMAN *driving, looks up.*

31   *Angle—Her Point of View: The doe looking huge through the windshield.*

32   *Angle: The doe's feet try to run on the icy surface of the road.*

33   *Angle:* NED *and* JIM *look away. The SOUND of a huge crash. Pause.* NED *and* JIM *look up.*

34   *Angle:* NED *and* JIM *walking over to the car.*

35   *Angle: The car, the dying doe under its wheels. The* OLD WOMAN *behind the wheel.* NED *and* JIM *walk over to her. Pause.*

NED: Hello . . . !

OLD WOMAN: *I'm* all right, I'm all right. Help me out of here.

They help her out of the car.

OLD WOMAN: Prob'ly wrecked the damn car . . . Prob'ly cost me every cent I have . . .

NED *looks at something.*

36   *Point of View Angle: An old side-by-side shotgun on the backseat.*

OLD WOMAN (*voice-over*): Prob'ly threw my *back* out . . . Oh hell . . .

37   *Angle: The three of them looking down at the deer.*

OLD WOMAN: What in the hell *you* doin' here on the road?

NED: We're looking for a ride into town.

OLD WOMAN: Are you indeed. Why should I give you one? I don't know who the hell you are. . . .

NED: We're going down to town to see the Shrine.

OLD WOMAN: You prob'ly scared the damn deer out into the road. What're you doing in the woods? Who are you?

Pause.

JIM: "Do not neglect to show hospitality to strangers, for thereby some have entertained angels unawares." Hebrews thirteen: one.

38   *Angle:* OLD WOMAN *looking at them.*

39   *Angle—Her Point of View: The dark coats over the doctors' smocks make them look as if they are wearing clerical collars.*

40   *Angle: The three.*

OLD WOMAN: What are you, priests?

NED: That's right.

OLD WOMAN: Well, you help me move the deer, I'll give you a ride. (*The car starts.*)

The OLD WOMAN *goes back into the car, comes out with the shotgun, hands it to* NED.

OLD WOMAN (*to herself*): Stay away, or he'll kick you to death.

41   Close-up: JIM *looking at the doe.*

42   Point of View: The doe's head. Large, terrified eyes.

43   Close-up: JIM *looking down. He looks to the side.* NED *points the shotgun at the doe, fires. Then he quickly points the barrel at the chains between their legs, fires again. The chain shatters.*

43A   Angle: NED *looks at* JIM.

JIM (*sotto*): Whatta we going to do about the old broad?

NED: She thinks we're priests.

He hands the shotgun back to her, and she puts it in the gun rack.

NED (*sotto to* JIM): Yeah, we brought a little religion into that broad's life. . . .

44   Interior: Car/Country Road—Day.

NED, *with a bandanna, trying to clean the blood off his clothes,* JIM *beside him.*

NED (*sotto*): . . . into the town, across the bridge, and we're free.

OLD WOMAN (*offscreen*): I'm sure they're looking for you.

NED *turns to her.*

NED: What . . . ?

45   Angle: The three of them.

OLD WOMAN: I'm sure they're looking for you.

NED: Who's looking for us?

OLD WOMAN: At the monastery. Your fellow priests.

NED: Yes, I'm sure they're looking for us.

OLD WOMAN: What are you, missing morning prayers?

NED: Yeah, we're missing the whole program, what do you care . . . ?

OLD WOMAN: I don't care a damn thing, I tol' you, it's all superstition, far as I'm concerned.

NED: That's fine. Now you just drop us in the town. . . .

OLD WOMAN: And I'll tell you what else, get people worked up . . .

She turns to the backseat to talk to them.

OLD WOMAN: Get people worked up over that *Shrine* of yours . . . "The Weeping Virgin."

46   Exterior: Town—Day.

> *Angle: The town which they are just entering, coming down a hill, a small bridge, two border checkpoints on either end.*

47   Angle: The three passengers in the car.

NED: We'll get out here.

OLD WOMAN: Won't be one more minute, I'll have you down.

NED: No, we'll get out here.

OLD WOMAN: Well, I could use your help, carry my deer to the butcher.

She stops the car.

NED: I tell you what, you go down, we'll meet you at the garage, carry your deer for you.

OLD WOMAN: Whyn't you just come down with me?

NED: I think we need a moment to compose our thoughts.

OLD WOMAN: Weren't for you I never'd'a killed that deer.

NED: Uh-huh. Well, thank you for your courtesy. God bless you, and all that.

NED *and* JIM *get out of the car.*

48   *Exterior: Town Square—Day.*

   The doe seen in the back, the two convicts get out. The car drives off. They look across the river.

49   *Exterior: Shantytown—Riverbank—Day.*

   Their Point of View: The bridge. The far side of the river.

50   *Angle: The two convicts.*

NED: Can you swim, Jimmy?

JIM: No.

NED: Me neither. Come on.

CAMERA FOLLOWS them down the hill through the beginning

of the small town. NED *stops in front of a window, looks at his reflection.*

JIM: You think Bob made it?

NED: Not looking like this he didn't; we're covered in blood. . . . Come on, we got to ditch these togs.

50A   *Exterior: Shantytown—Boardwalk—Day.*

> *CAMERA FOLLOWS them around to the back of a house. Rows of laundry stretch from the houses before them.*

JIM: Whaddaya gonna do on Free Street, Neddy?

NED: I'm gonna do it all, pal. (*Beat.*) And then I'm gonna do it again—and I'm gonna get two the best of everything— and anybody muck with me is going down.

CAMERA FOLLOWS them as they start taking the laundry off the various lines. They hungrily dress themselves in the warm clothes. NED *moves on, dressing himself, offscreen.* JIMMY *stops, looking at something.*

51   *Point of View: The window beyond the line. A mother is serving breakfast to two little kids, hugging them.*

52   *Close-up:* JIM's *face, wistful.*

53   *Angle:* NED *moves down the line, dressing himself. He takes down a shirt, sees something beyond it.*

54   *Point of View: Another window. A beautiful naked young woman, heating water at her stove, pours it into her washbowl. She ties her hair up with a large yellow ribbon, starts washing her face. This is* MOLLY.

JIM (*offscreen*): Maan, what I wouldn't give, what I wouldn't give . . .

55   *Angle:* NED *looks at the naked young woman.* JIM *looks in the opposite direction, putting on a vest he has just taken down from the line.*

JIM: What I wouldn't give for a *cigarette.* . . .

NED (*turning away*): Let's get out of here. . . .

55A   *Exterior: Town Square—Alley—Day.*

The two men move down Main Street to alley between hotel and barbershop. NED *plucks down a heavy woolen overshirt. They stop. Beyond them, traffic just starting to move. They stand in the shade of the alley. A monk driving a tractor passes by.*

NED: You ready . . . ?

JIM: I wonder what happened to Bob, I wonder did he get across. . . .

NED: What happened to him happened to him, Jim.

JIM: Maybe they got him back, but *I'm not* going back there.

NED: That's right. We're not going back.

JIM: We look, hey, we look like a couple of Hoosiers. . . .

NED: That's right. Let's go.

They start out into the street. JIM *sees something, motions* NED *to stop. He scampers up a short staircase and puts on a heavy woolen coat hanging on a peg outside* SHOPKEEPER's *back door. He comes down.*

JIM: Okay; let's go. . . .

As they walk out, they pass under a banner across the street. It reads, CELEBRATE THE FEAST OF OUR LADY OF THE SORROWS.

56   *Exterior: Town Square—Day.*

       The two convicts come out onto the street. They walk purposefully forward.

57   *Their Point of View: The bridge. Up ahead, the customs shed, the barrier.*

58   *Angle: The convicts.* JIM *starts to whistle. He jingles coins.*

JIM (*producing coins from his pocket*): Hey, coins in the pocket, that's good luck. That's good luck, don't you think . . . ?

JIMMY *sees something before him.*

59   *Point of View: The* SHERIFF *walking over to the customs shed, distributing leaflets.*

JIM (*offscreen*): Oh, God, oh, God . . .

60   *Angle:* JIMMY *and* NED.

NED: It's okay; it's going to be okay.

A drayman is coming up the street in his horse-drawn truck. He CRACKS *the whip over the horse.* JIM *winces; his hand goes to rub his back.*

JIM: I'm not going back, Ned.

NED: Nobody's going back. It's going to be fine.

JIM *wipes his forehead.*

JIM: I need a smoke, Ned, I'm telling you. . . .

NED: Okay. We'll get you a smoke, and then we go across.

JIM: You'll take care of me, Ned, 'cause I got to get across.

NED: Just keep walking. . . .

They veer off in their progress toward the bridge. CAMERA FOL-LOWS them to the sidewall, to a general store. The owner, inside, is just seen turning the CLOSED *sign to* OPEN.

61   *Interior: General Store—Day.*

   NED *and* JIM *enter. The* SHOPKEEPER *is in the back with a customer.*

SHOPKEEPER (*looking up*): Right with you.

JIM, *looking nervous, nudges* NED. NED *looks.*

62   *Point of View: A wanted notice tacked on the wall behind a display, with three crudely drawn faces on it, the same poster the sheriff was distributing earlier.*

63   *Angle:* NED *and* JIM.

NED (*to* SHOPKEEPER): Just a pack of tailor-mades . . .

SHOPKEEPER: Right with you.

JIM *looks out the window.*

64   *Point of View: The border crossing. The sheriff's deputies look intently at people going across.*

65   *Angle:* JIM *turns back to the store. He and* NED *look down; something catches their interest.*

66   *Point of View: The display counter full of handguns, a Colt display.*

67   *Angle:* JIM *looks at* NED, *catches his eye, then looks at the guns again.*

SHOPKEEPER (*offscreen*): Buncha nonsense, all them damn *priests* in towns, the Shrine, don't buy a damn *thing,* but they *want* something, you better have it on hand. . . . I'll be with you gents in a second.

NED: We just want a packet of smokes. . . .

JIM *turns his back on the* SHOPKEEPER, *slides toward the guns. He picks up a promotional pamphlet off the top of the counter. Holds it up. It reads* Colt on the Trail. *It has pictures of revolvers on the cover. He opens it, reads, "Have you ever been completely alone, with no one to rely on . . . ?"*

SHOPKEEPER (*offscreen*): Mementos of the *Shrine, postcards . . .*

68   *Angle: The* SHOPKEEPER *opens a carton of souvenirs. He holds one up.*

SHOPKEEPER: Key chains of the Weeping Virgin . . . not a penny in it, but they want it every year, priests and the tourists . . . put on that dumb show.

SOUND of the shop bell ringing. MOLLY, *the girl with the yellow ribbon in her hair, enters the store. Walks past* NED, *over to the counter. She picks up two containers of oatmeal.*

MOLLY (*to the* SHOPKEEPER): Two packages oatmeal, set it down, will you?

SHOPKEEPER: Account's gettin' a bit *long.* . . .

MOLLY: Well, I *need* it, set it down.

SHOPKEEPER: . . . Uh . . .

MOLLY: I got a hungry kid. You'll catch me later.

She picks up the two packages, starts out of the store. NED is looking at her.

MOLLY: What're *you* looking at?

He holds up his hands—i.e., "No offense."

MOLLY: . . . That's *right*. . . .

She exits.

SHOPKEEPER (*to* NED): Special kind of smokes?

He turns back.

NED: Camel's'll do. . . .

SHOPKEEPER: The Shrine, talking about it. Didn't mean to offend you, now 'n' I probably put my foot in it 'n' you're tourists, come to see the Shrine. . . .

Beat. CAMERA PANS WITH the SHOPKEEPER *as he turns to the cigarette display, picks a pack of smokes out of it, and stops. Tacked next to the cigarette display is the wanted poster. Beat.*

SHOPKEEPER: . . . Where *are* you folks from . . . ?

The SHOPKEEPER *turns with the smokes to* NED; JIM *is in the background, with the pamphlet, trying to reach behind to steal a gun.*

NED: Oh, here and there . . .

SHOPKEEPER (*to* JIM): Something I can interest you in that case . . . ?

He walks over to JIM.

NED: Oh, we should be 'bout going. . . .

NED *pays for the smokes.*

NED (*to* JIM): . . . We should be 'bout going now. . . .

JIM *folds the pamphlet, puts it into his coat; they start to edge toward the door.*

SHOPKEEPER: You forgot your change.

NED: Oh, that's okay. . . .

At the door they freeze.

69   *Point of View: The* SHERIFF *outside the door, talking to his deputy.*

70   *Angle: The two turning back toward the* SHOPKEEPER.

NED: Yessir, *change.* Lessee if we can't spend it in your store.

The SHOPKEEPER *hands the change to* NED.

SHOPKEEPER: You folks hear about the jailbreak . . . ?

NED: No, I can't say that we have.

Pause. The SHOPKEEPER *looks at them. He looks at the poster.*

SHOPKEEPER: Where'd you say you were from . . . ?

71 *Close-up:* NED. *He looks outside. The* SHERIFF *is right out-side the door.*

72 *Angle:* NED *looks at* JIM. JIM *starts to edge toward the gun case.*

73 *Angle: The* SHOPKEEPER, *behind the counter, edges toward a pistol lying on a low shelf.*

SHOPKEEPER: Yessir, it seems there were these three *convicts* . . . shot their way out. . . .

He starts to pick up the gun. We hear DOORBELL JINGLING.

OLD WOMAN (*offscreen*): *There* you are.

74 *Angle: The* OLD WOMAN *has just come into the shop.*

OLD WOMAN: I *told* you I needed your help.

SHOPKEEPER: These friends of yours . . . ?

NED: . . . my help . . . ?

OLD WOMAN: My car's stalled, down at the garage, 'n' I need you to haul that deer down to the *butchers.*

SHOPKEEPER: You know these folks?

OLD WOMAN: Know 'em, yeah, they're *priests.* This is Father . . . I didn't catch your name. . . .

SHOPKEEPER: Priests? Oh, God, oh, God, I'm sorry. I'm sorry, what I'm saying . . . gentlemen, Father, ramblin' on, and now I've offended you. No, no, no hard feelings. . . .

NED: That's fine.

OLD WOMAN: You going to help me with that deer . . . ?

SHOPKEEPER: I mean, I'die 'f I thought I *offended* you . . .

NED: No, we'll forget it.

SHOPKEEPER: Or *anyone* associated with the Shrine . . .

He comes around the corner, picks up handfuls of Shrine key chains, and presses them on NED *and* JIM.

SHOPKEEPER: Well, here, little token. Take 'em . . . please take some back for your friends, we got the Shrine on one side, 'n' a thermometer on the other. . . .

75   *Insert: The key chain. It shows the Shrine of the Weeping Virgin.* NED *turns it over in his hand, and we see the thermometer.*

76   *Angle: The* OLD WOMAN, *ushering the two convicts out the door.*

SHOPKEEPER: Awfully handy, really. (*He glances at the thermometer.*) Cool day today! Button up!

He waves.

JIM: Yes, indeed.

SHOPKEEPER (*smiling*): No hard feelings . . . Father . . .

JIM: Go with God.

SHOPKEEPER (*pointing at* JIM): I have that same coat!

They all smile at each other cheerily. The OLD WOMAN *turns back to the* SHOPKEEPER, *hands him a piece of paper.*

OLD WOMAN: Harry, here's a list, and I'll also need a few shells for that old twelve-gauge.

The three start out of the door.

77   *Exterior: Town Square—Day.*

   The three walking down the street.

OLD WOMAN: Damn car's all stove in, need a new radiator, how'm I going to afford that . . . ? I should turn in a bill to your *church*, I swear to God.

NED: Why don't you . . . ?

OLD WOMAN: Everything so expensive . . . canned goods.

They pass by a wanted poster, showing the faces of the three wanted convicts. They come up to the garage. In the background, the car, with the deer in it.

OLD WOMAN: . . . Cheaper to shop in Canada . . .

NED: Well, why *don't* you . . . ?

OLD WOMAN: I *would*, 'cept my car's wrecked, 'n' I walk *over*, how'm I going to get my groceries back?

NED *looks over at the border.*

78   *Point of View: Several people lined up to get across, being interrogated by the* DEPUTY.

79   *Angle:* NED, JIM, *the* OLD WOMAN.

NED: After what you've done for us, we'll go with you and fetch your things back.

They change their course and walk toward the border.

OLD WOMAN: That's very Christian of you.

JIM: Well, you know what it says in the Bible . . .

OLD WOMAN: What's that?

JIM: *You* know . . .

OLD WOMAN: Matter of fact, I usually *do* my shopping over there, though I wouldn't let on to Harry. You think that's dishonesty, you just go on and *think* it. . . .

They draw closer to the border. JIM *begins to look afraid. He leans down to hitch up his leg iron; the chains CLINK as he does it.*

JIM (*sotto, to* NED): I can't do it.

NED (*sotto*): Yes, you can, Jim. It's a piece of cake.

JIM (*sotto*): I can't do it.

NED (*sotto*): Now, you want to kill yourself, that's fine. But there's two of us here, 'n' I'm counting on you, so you buck up, Jimmy, 'n' you act like a priest.

They look toward the border.

80   *Point of View: The border guard checking faces against the wanted poster.*

81   *Insert:* JIM's *hand takes the key chain out of his pocket.*

JIM (*offscreen, very softly*): . . . Hail Mary, full of grace . . .

He holds the key chain like a rosary and continues with his prayer as they approach the border.

DEPUTY (*offscreen*): Morning, ma'am.

OLD WOMAN (*offscreen*): How are you today, you working hard . . . ?

DEPUTY (*offscreen*): Well, we're looking for those *convicts* escaped . . .

82   *Angle:* JIM *watches the* DEPUTY *walk the* OLD WOMAN *toward the border.* NED *reaches into the* OLD WOMAN's *shopping bag, takes out her spectacles, puts them on.* JIM *pulls his hat down lower.*

OLD WOMAN: Convicts, convicts . . . Oh! I found them for you!

JIM *and* NED *are at the border, scared.*

OLD WOMAN: I found them for you!

JIM *and* NED *look trapped.* JIM *looks at the* BORDER GUARD *with a shotgun.* NED *turns his head.*

83   *Exterior: Canadian Customs/Border—Day.*

His Point of View.

84   *Angle:* NED *hangs his head.*

OLD WOMAN (*offscreen*): Come *over* here, I found your lost ones . . . !

85   *Angle: The border station. The two convicts and the* OLD WOMAN, *who has just corralled an old priest in long skirts who is carrying a shopping bag.*

OLD WOMAN: You see, you see, they were lost and I found them.

FATHER LEVESQUE (*old priest*): Good morning, Caroline, you found whom?

OLD WOMAN: Your two lost priests. (*Pause.*) I found your lost priests.

FATHER LEVESQUE *stares at the two. Beat.*

FATHER LEVESQUE: Where have you been?

Beat.

JIM: Uh, well, *you* know . . .

NED: We were . . .

FATHER LEVESQUE: We wired *Arizona* . . . Your Monsignor . . . where have you *been* . . . ?

JIM: . . . We got misplaced.

They have reached the front of the border and are about to be examined by the SHERIFF *and the* DEPUTY.

FATHER LEVESQUE: Sheriff, do you know who these are . . . ? Mrs. Blair found Father Brown and Father Riley . . . !

DEPUTY: Thank the Lord, we thought maybe the convicts got you.

NED: Convicts . . . ?

SHERIFF: Had a jailbreak. Got me some *killers* on the loose . . .

The SHERIFF *waves away the customs agent checking everyone as he begins to walk the group across the bridge.*

SHERIFF (*to deputies*): That's all right, boys . . .

CAMERA FOLLOWS them across the bridge.

FATHER LEVESQUE: But where have you been, and where are your clothes . . . ?

JIM: They got lost when the, *you* know . . .

OLD WOMAN: I found them like this coming through the woods. Looked like a couple of raggle-taggle gypsies.

FATHER LEVESQUE: Gypsies? Do you know who these *are?* This is Fathers Brown and Riley, Brown and Riley, *A New Look at Deuteronomy.*

SHERIFF: Uh-huh . . .

86   Angle: NED *and* JIM.

87   Their Point of View: Canadian Customs/Border fast approaching.

FATHER LEVESQUE (*offscreen*): These are two of the finest thinkers in the church today.

88   Angle: The group almost at the Canadian side.

DEPUTY: Pleasure, waal, a real *pleasure,* and you-all got lost in the woods, right? (*Shakes hands with them.*) Waiting for you folks two days . . .

FATHER LEVESQUE: That's right.

NED: Yes.

We hear a CLANK. Beat. NED *bends down as if to tie his shoelace. He reties his chain to his calf, ties his shoelace.*

SHERIFF: Lucky, you say you were lost in the woods? Lucky one of our *boys* didn't get on to you, 'n' take you for the *convicts.* . . .

NED *straightens up.*

NED: What would they have done . . . ?

SHERIFF: Done . . . would of *shot* you.

FATHER LEVESQUE: We've been meeting every train for the last two days. . . .

89   *Exterior: Canadian Customs/Border—Day.*

> *Angle: The barrier. The far side manned by Mounties. The group reaches the barrier. A Mountie guard comes forward.*

SHERIFF (*to the Mounties*): That's all right, boys, let 'em across.

The barrier starts to raise.

90   *Angle:* NED *and* JIM *smile.*

FATHER LEVESQUE: It wasn't going to be a convocation *without* you. . . .

The OLD WOMAN *and the priests are about to cross into Canada.*

SHERIFF: You have a good day, Mrs. Blair. . . .

91   *Angle: The feet of the convicts about to cross the line on the bridge separating the two countries.*

FATHER LEVESQUE: Well, we'd best be getting back. . . .

92   *Exterior: Bridge—Day.*

*Angle: He starts to turn back, taking the two convicts by the
arm. The* DEPUTY *starts back with them. The two convicts
strain toward Canada.*

JIM: We have to help Mrs. Blair with her groceries.

OLD WOMAN: Well, now, you've just betrayed a *trust, haven't*
you . . . ?

DEPUTY (*to one of the deputies*): George, run along over with
Caroline, and help her with her shopping.

NED: I'd really rather *we* went, we did *promise* the broad . . .

FATHER LEVESQUE: No, no, no, we're all so *anxious* for you . . .
come on, now. . . .

They all walk back toward the American border.

SHERIFF: Father Levesque, I'll want to come by later, talk
about the plans for the Procession.

FATHER LEVESQUE: Anytime.

SHERIFF: Sorry I haven't been by before, but with this *prison*
escape . . .

FATHER LEVESQUE: Believe me, I understand.

SHERIFF: So, I'll be by sometime today, and of course, I'll be
on duty for the Procession of the Shrine.

SHERIFF (*over his shoulder to a deputy*): Any males come
through here, the right age, you pat 'em down, pat 'em right
down for the *leg* irons.

He starts to demonstrate on the deputy. Then moves on to demon-strate on NED.

SHERIFF: *Right* down, knees to their ankles, 'n' don't be bashful . . .

NED *moves over to the side of the bridge. Looks out over the water.*

NED: Wasn't that a cormorant . . . ?

SHERIFF: And I mean you check *everybody*.

They move on through, back to the American side.

FATHER LEVESQUE: You think they'll come through this way?

SHERIFF: Got to. Come through, swim the river 'n' drown, or die in the woods. *We'll* get 'em. (*Tips his hat.*) Gentlemen.

The Father takes the two convicts and moves off. CAMERA FOL-LOWS.

FATHER LEVESQUE: I thank the Lord that you've come. We've been praying for your safety for two days.

JIM: That's very nice of you.

FATHER LEVESQUE: You know, I wouldn't have recognized you from your pictures. . . .

NED: Well, you know, we've, uh, we've uh . . .

JIM: We had to change somewhat because of the things that happened to us.

FATHER LEVESQUE: And *what* happened to your clothes . . . ?

JIM: They got lost when the *thing* happened.

NED *looks back over his shoulder.*

93   *Exterior: Canadian Customs/Border—Day.*

Point of View: The far side, Canada retreating.

94   *Exterior: Blacksmith Shop—Day.*

Angle: The group walking down the street.

FATHER LEVESQUE: Well, we'll get your vestments and all at the monastery.

NED: Thank you, we'd appreciate that.

FATHER LEVESQUE: We wired Arizona when you didn't arrive on time, but they said they had no clue. Your Monsignor's *quite* worried. And then, the *snow,* and then these *prisoners . . .*

JIM: I'll tell you something, nothing was going to stop us from coming here.

We hear the SOUNDS of their chains clinking. JIM *reaches down and adjusts his chain. They pass by a blacksmith shop. We hear the HAMMER hitting the forge.* JIM *and* NED *look at the blacksmith's shop.*

95   *Exterior: Monastery—Day.*

Point of View: The blacksmith hitting the anvil.

FATHER LEVESQUE (*offscreen*): Shall we go in . . . ?

96   *Angle: The group has arrived at the steps of the monastery.* FATHER LEVESQUE *starts up the stairs.* NED *leans over to* JIM. *They whisper.*

NED (*sotto*): Get these chains knocked off at the blacksmith's shop, get into these priest duds, 'n' back over the border.

JIM (*sotto*): You call it, Neddy. . . .

FATHER LEVESQUE (*offscreen*): Coming . . . ?

97 *Interior: Monastery—Chapel—Day.*

> *Angle: They start up the stairs into the monastery. CAMERA FOLLOWS them into the church portion of the monastery. Before them is the Shrine of the Madonna. FATHER LE-VESQUE crosses himself. The two convicts, awkwardly, do likewise. FATHER LEVESQUE turns to them.*

FATHER LEVESQUE: I know this must be quite a moment for you. (*Beat.*) To've written so much about the Shrine, but never to've *seen* her.

FATHER LEVESQUE *turns to look at the Shrine. The two priests do likewise.*

98 *Point of View: The statue of the Madonna.*

FATHER LEVESQUE (*offscreen*): That's why I took you back from the border.

99 *Angle: The group.*

FATHER LEVESQUE: I knew how much you wanted to be here.

Beat.

NED: Thank you.

FATHER LEVESQUE: . . . the weeping Madonna.

FATHER LEVESQUE *sighs, turns. The two convicts follow him.*

99A   Interior: Monastery—Vestry—Day.

FATHER LEVESQUE *gestures them in.*

FATHER LEVESQUE: You'll find some cassocks in here.

He exits, leaving them to it. NED *and* JIM *change into priests' clothes. A* YOUNG MONK *peeps through the door.*

YOUNG MONK: Father, Father.

He beckons them to follow. CAMERA FOLLOWS.

YOUNG MONK: We've been waiting for you. Eagerly. We *prayed* for you. . . .

NED: We were delayed.

YOUNG MONK (*confidentially*): I've read all your books.

NED: Thank you.

YOUNG MONK: You know, you don't look a *thing* like your pictures.

He removes a book from his cassock.

100   Insert: The Book. A New Look at Deuteronomy, *"by Frs. Brown and Riley." The book is turned over, and we see two heavyset priests standing in the sun. One wears a cowboy hat.*

101   Angle: NED *takes the book away.*

NED (*of the photograph*): Fasting and prayer.

YOUNG MONK: It's such an honor to have men of your learning, of your reputation here. . . . We were so worried about you. . . .

JIM: Mmmm.

YOUNG MONK: We wired the diocese in Arizona.

NED: Yeah. He told us. We appreciate it.

YOUNG MONK: Well, thank the Lord you've come. . . .

The YOUNG MONK *puts his hand on* JIM's *back. The* YOUNG MONK *looks surprised, feels in the back of the collar of* JIM's *coat.*

YOUNG MONK: What's *this* . . . ?

102   *Angle: The* YOUNG MONK *and* JIM. *The* YOUNG MONK *produces a clothespin from the back of* JIM's *coat collar. Beat.*

JIM: You don't know what that is?

YOUNG MONK: No.

JIM: It's a clothespin.

102A   *Interior: Monastery—Chapel—Day.*

YOUNG MONK *leads* JIM *and* NED *toward refectory door.*

YOUNG MONK: Father, why are you wearing it in your collar?

JIM: Aha. (*Pause.*) The thing of it *is* . . . you know what it is . . . ?

YOUNG MONK: . . . No.

JIM: It is a . . . *reminder, any* of us, could get snatched at any moment.

102B   Interior: Monastery—Refectory—Day.

The YOUNG MONK *hesitates, nods in appreciation. We hear the assembled monks CHANT a phrase in unison.*

NED *sits near* FATHER LEVESQUE *at the head table. Jim sits beside him. The monks stop chanting.* FATHER LEVESQUE *intones a Latin incantation. The assemblage bow their heads in silence, then respond.* JIM *and* NED *bow their heads.* JIM *looks to* NED; NED *shrugs and begins to mumble. They all mumble.*

FATHER LEVESQUE *says, "Amen." Beat.* NED *and* JIM *begin to reach for the food.*

FATHER LEVESQUE: And I would like to add one *special* prayer. Of thanksgiving . . .

NED *and* JIM *draw back. Wait.*

FATHER LEVESQUE: All my friends, and guests here tonight, a special prayer of thanksgiving for the safe arrival of Father Riley and Father Brown. Many of us are acquainted with their works, and we are all, I am sure, glad of the opportunity to meet them in person.

JIM *begins to stand, as if to receive an accolade.* NED *drags him back down.*

FATHER LEVESQUE: We are thankful for their presence, for their scholarship, for the participation in the Procession of the Shrine. A special prayer, tonight, from the Old Testament, Leviticus three: thirteen.

NED *and* JIM *bow their heads.*

FATHER LEVESQUE: Father Brown, would you render it for us . . . ?

Beat.

103   *Angle:* NED *and* JIM. *Their heads bowed. They realize that it is they who are being addressed. They begin to look anxious.*

104   *Close-up: The two whispering, simultaneously.*

NED/JIM: I think *you're* Brown.

They try to push each other up. NED *finally pushes up* JIM. JIM *stands, looks around.*

105   *Point of View: A sea of expectant faces.*

106   *Angle: At the top of the table, the* YUGOSLAV PRIEST *and his* TRANSLATOR *begin speaking to* FATHER LEVESQUE. *The* YUGOSLAV PRIEST *speaks; the* TRANSLATOR *translates.*

TRANSLATOR: Father Nogulich points out it is *his* turn to read the grace.

FATHER LEVESQUE: We appreciate your courtesy in ceding your place to our new arrivals.

JIM: Let 'em read it, it's his *turn.* I don't wanna get in anyone's *face* here. . . .

FATHER LEVESQUE: No, Father Brown. Please. Honor us. Leviticus three: thirteen.

JIM *sweats. He looks around at the sea of expectant faces, then at* NED. NED *looks up as if to say, "I can't help you."* JIM *looks around, sees something. Looks back at* NED, *smiles, looks in the direction of his salvation.*

107   *Angle: The* YOUNG MONK *is bringing him the Bible.* JIM *smiles, takes the Bible. Clears his throat. Looks down. Beat. Blanches.*

108   *Point of View: The book. It is in Latin.*

109   *Angle:* JIM *is terrified. Looks around. Looks down at the book. Beat.* JIM *closes the book.*

JIM: You know what? Let's just say something *appropriate. Here's* a good grace: Be nice to strangers, because sometimes *you're* a stranger too.

He smiles.

The YOUNG MONK *is fully appreciative, thoughtful:* "There's *a novel thought."*

FATHER LEVESQUE *intones,* "Amen"; *the chorus of monks responds. The* YUGOSLAV PRIEST *speaks to the* TRANSLATOR, *who leans over and speaks to* FATHER LEVESQUE.

TRANSLATOR: This is not a fitting grace. . . .

FATHER LEVESQUE: A little unusual, *quite* to the point, I thought.

TRANSLATOR: What are we, *Protestants* . . . ?

110   *Angle:* JIM *sits, nods as if to say "Well,* there's *one grace that got said correctly." He starts to eat.*

111   *Interior: Monastery—The Refectory Hall—Day.*

The last remnants of food being cleared away by some monks, the remainder of the monks bent over prayer books.

112 *Angle:* NED *and* JIM, *their heads bent over their books. Beat.* NED *leans over and whispers.*

NED (*sotto*): As soon as we pop off the ankles . . . you listening to me?

JIM *gives him a look, remonstrating with him, then inclines his head toward his prayer book, as if to say, "Can't you see I'm studying . . . ?" Beat.* NED *looks at him, looks around the hall.*

113 *Point of View: The monks bent over their books. At the high table* FATHER LEVESQUE *closes his books and says, "Amen."*

114 *Angle: Ned and Jim's table. All the monks say, "Amen."* JIM *keeps reading.*

115 *Angle: Over* JIM'S *shoulder. The prayer book in Latin, within which he has secreted the Colt firearms pamphlet. On the page he is reading is a picture of a black native in a loincloth being held at bay by a sahib, who is shielding a terrified white woman. The headline is "Saved from a Fate Worse Than Death."*

NED (*offscreen*): Jimmy, get out of it, will you . . . ?

116 *Angle: The table. All the priests and monks get up; several nod at the two.* JIM *folds up his book, slips the pamphlet back into his coat.*

NED: You lay low here for a while, I'm gonna find some way to pop us out of these chains, and then we head across the river.

JIM: We're safe stayin' right here, Ned.

NED: Yeah; till the real priests show up, we're safe. . . .

JIM: Oh.

They get up and start to file out of the hall along with the rest of the monks. The YUGOSLAV PRIEST *and his* TRANSLATOR *come by.*

TRANSLATOR: The father says he has read your book. *A New Look at Deuteronomy.*

NED: Yeah, what'd he think of it?

TRANSLATOR: He found your theology amusing, and wondered if you intended it as such.

The TRANSLATOR *smirks.*

NED: Well, who did *he* ever fight . . . ?

FATHER LEVESQUE *comes by.*

FATHER LEVESQUE: I hope you'll participate in our lectures later on the Shrine.

JIM: I'd like nothing better.

The two veer off into a deserted hallway; CAMERA FOLLOWS.

117   *Exterior: Monastery—Day.*

> *The banner reading,* HELP RESTORE THE SHRINE OF ST. ANN, *through the archway, in the refectory. Monks clearing the tables.* NED *and* JIM *come out of the refectory, picking their teeth.*

NED: We get these leg chains off, then straight across the river. . . . You lay low around here, half an hour, meet you right back here.

YOUNG MONK (*offscreen*): Father Brown . . . !

JIM (*sotto*): Who's Brown . . . ?

NED: *You* are. . . .

The YOUNG MONK *comes up to them, holds a large fishbowl.*

YOUNG MONK: Shall I enter your name in the lottery?

NED *nods, moves off.*

JIM: What's the prize? Hey, don't bother. Well, no, I never won anything.

YOUNG MONK: You can never tell! I'll put you down.

The YOUNG MONK *starts away, turns back, catches* JIM's *eyes. The* YOUNG MONK *shows* JIM *the back of his collar. On it is attached a clothespin. He winks at* JIM, *as if to say, "I got the message. . . ."*

118   *Interior: Blacksmith Shop—Day.*

> *Dark shadows. We hear the CLANKING of the hammer on the forge.* NED *comes INTO THE FRAME, sneaking. CAMERA PULLS BACK SLIGHTLY to reveal we are in a blacksmith shop.* NED *looks around the wall nearest him, on which tools hang. He finds small clippers and takes them down off the wall. He bends down and tries to sever his leg manacle with the small clippers. It is too small to do the trick. He rises up, looks around.*

119   *Point of View: Very large clippers across the shop on the wall. CAMERA CONTINUES to the* BLACKSMITH, *at the anvil, with his back to* NED.

120   *Angle:* NED *sneaks across the shop. He gets the clippers. He looks around and starts back toward the door into the cloisters.*

VOICE (*offscreen*): Afternoon, Bill.

BLACKSMITH (*offscreen*): Sheriff . . .

NED *freezes.*

SHERIFF (*offscreen*): I'm going to need them horses back this afternoon.

BLACKSMITH (*offscreen*): You goin' back up in the hills?

SHERIFF (*offscreen*): Well, they got to be somewhere, got no food, prison *clothes;* either they're up there in the woods or they're going to try to cross over here.

BLACKSMITH (*offscreen*): You get the bridge staked out pretty good, do you?

SHERIFF (*offscreen*): You best believe we do. We're bringing out the *dogs.* Dogs'll be here any minute. We've got the prison *staff* come down, stand guard on the bridge with us. Oh, we'll catch 'em, don't worry.

BLACKSMITH (*offscreen*): Bring 'em back whichever way they want . . .

NED *is trying to edge along the wall to the door in the back wall.*

SHERIFF (*offscreen*): Y'ask me, though, I think it'd be a lot less problem shoot to kill.

BLACKSMITH (*offscreen*): Uh-huh . . .

SHERIFF (*offscreen*): I think that's the Bible, isn't it . . . ? They killed and they shall be killed . . . ?

NED *dislodges a harness from the wall. It falls noisily.*

121   *Point of View: The* SHERIFF *and the* BLACKSMITH *turning.*
        The SHERIFF *in the process of tacking up the wanted poster.*

SHERIFF: What was that?

BLACKSMITH: Well, I don't *know.* . . .

The SHERIFF *starts toward the CAMERA.*

122   *Angle:* NED *cowers down in the stall. The* SHERIFF, *in the*
        background, coming closer, sure to find him. NED *hangs his*
        head, prays, sees something.

123   *Point of View: A cat.*

124   *Angle:* NED *picks up the cat, throws it out of the stall.*

125   *Angle: The cat runs past the* SHERIFF. *He turns his head.*

SHERIFF: *Here* she goes . . . !

In the background we see NED *slipping out the back door into the*
monastery.

126   *Interior: Monastery Chapel—Day.*

        NED *enters, holding the heavy clippers down along his leg,*
        looking for a place to remove his chains.

        Walks toward an alcove, CAMERA FOLLOWS. He gets to
        the alcove, and there is a monk in it, praying. NED *looks*
        around, starts walking. CAMERA FOLLOWS him into the
        nave of the church. It is empty. NED *looks around, walks to*
        the confessional box, peeks back toward the hall.

127   *Point of View: The empty chapel.*

128   *Angle:* NED *looks around. He hides in the confessional.*

129   *Interior: The Confessional.*

NED *crouches. The SOUND of heavy footsteps, coming closer.* NED *crouches down. He holds on to the clippers as if they were a weapon. The footsteps draw closer. We hear the opposite door of the confessional OPENING.*

DEPUTY (*offscreen*): Father, forgive me, for I have sinned, it has been three weeks since my last confession. . . .

Confessional stuff etc., as NED *tries to remember the form etc. Pause.*

NED: Uhhh.

DEPUTY: And I can't *help* myself. . . .

NED: Uh.

DEPUTY: Please, please.

NED: Well, *what* . . . ?

DEPUTY: *Help* me.

As NED *speaks, he tries to work the clippers.*

NED: *Okay,* what, what is it? (*Pause.*) I can't help you if you don't *tell* me.

Pause.

DEPUTY: I have been sleeping with this woman.

NED: All right, and what? You're not married to her?

DEPUTY: No.

NED: You're married to someone else?

DEPUTY: To my wife.

NED: Your wife know about this?

DEPUTY: No.

NED: Well, then, forget about it. Stop whining.

DEPUTY: But I broke my vow. I'm such a sinner. *Help* me.

NED: Okay, okay, look. Go make a good act of contrition, try to break off seeing this broad, say ten Hail Marys, and if you see the girl again, okay? Pop back here. No big deal.

He succeeds in breaking the manacles with a large POP. He smiles, puts the chains in his pocket, makes the sign of the cross.

NED: God bless you.

He exits the confessional with the large clippers.

130   Interior: Monastery—Chapel.

> *Angle:* NED *looking around for a place to stash the clippers. The* DEPUTY *comes out of the confessional, comes up toward* NED. NED, *alarmed, slips into a pew, kneels, slips the clippers under the pew. The* DEPUTY *kneels next to him.*

DEPUTY: I can't, Father, I can't help myself. *You* have to help me.

NED: Well, I did what I could. There's a time, a man has got to stand up, take a stand. Look, look, look, take a few days off, go in the woods, something, make your peace with God.

DEPUTY: I can't leave till we catch those convicts. I'm stuck here in town. I'm in constant temptation.

NED *gets up; the* DEPUTY *follows. The* DEPUTY *physically stops him.*

DEPUTY: Please help me, I can't control myself.

NED, *exasperated, looks around.*

131   Point of View: The Shrine of the Virgin, which they are standing under.

DEPUTY (*offscreen*): I need your help. *You're* a pious man, you're a good man, help me.

132   Angle: NED *and the* DEPUTY.

NED: How can I help you?

132A   Exterior: Monastery—Day.

> *They have come into the courtyard.* NED *sees* JIM *waiting for him.* NED *signs to* JIM: *"Just be patient."* JIM *nods.*

DEPUTY: Come with me, talk to her, talk to us together.

NED: Aw, *look,* buddy . . .

DEPUTY: I've dragged her in sin, too. . . .

NED: I'm sure that the young woman . . .

The DEPUTY *falls to his knees.*

DEPUTY: I'm begging you, Father.

NED: Get up.

DEPUTY: Father. I need your help.

NED: All right, all right, okay, okay, okay . . .

He is taken by the arm, and the two proceed across the courtyard. NED *looks back at* JIM. JIM *signs, "Okay, but hurry. . . ."* CAMERA STAYS *on* JIM. *We hear a dog BARKING.* JIM *looks.*

133   *Exterior: Monastery—Day.*

    Point of View: The SHERIFF *and a deputy leading the two bloodhounds.*

134   *Angle:* JIM *slowly gets up from his bench, walks slowly away from the bloodhounds.*

135   *Angle: The bloodhounds stop, sniff the air, start toward* JIM.

136   *Angle:* JIM *disappearing under the banner which says,* HELP RESTORE THE SHRINE OF ST. ANN.

137   *Exterior: Monastery/Shantytown/Molly's House—Day.*

    A raggedy GIRL *of five, a garbage can, in an ill-lit corner of the staircase. The* GIRL *is playing with various objects from the garbage. We hear* NED *and the* DEPUTY *COMING UP the stairs.*

DEPUTY: And I prayed, I prayed to the Blessed Virgin, I have prayed to St. Ann, and I ask, I *ask* myself . . . why, why am I so weak? Why am I *branded?*

NED: Okay. Okay. Calm down.

The priest stops in front of the door.

DEPUTY: And I say, Lord, Lord. I am a fornicator, strike me

down, strike me . . . what am I doing to myself and my wife?
I'm a *fornicator.* . . .

NED *shushes him. He nods toward the* LITTLE GIRL.

DEPUTY: She can't hear. The poor child's deaf and dumb.

NED *looks at the* LITTLE GIRL. *She is playing with the garbage.
The* DEPUTY *KNOCKS on the door. A woman's VOICE answers,
"Come in." The* DEPUTY *signals to* NED *to wait; he goes inside.
Beat.* NED *stands, looking at the door. He looks at the* LITTLE
GIRL. *The* LITTLE GIRL *looks at him and goes back to playing.*
NED *sighs. Paces around the stair landing. The chains he is hold-
ing CREAK. He looks around, deposits them in the garbage pail.
The door to the room opens; the* DEPUTY *calls* NED.

138   Interior: Molly's Room—Day.

> *A squalid room, cluttered, laundry hanging.* MOLLY, *a girl
> of twenty-two, in a slip, sitting on the bed, mending, smoking
> a cigarette.*

DEPUTY: I've brought this man here to avow our shame.

MOLLY *looks up.*

MOLLY: *I* don't care. . . .

DEPUTY: We . . .

MOLLY: Hey, I don't care, and I *told* you I don't care. You did
whatcha did, if you think that's a sin, you live with it. Now
I'm busy now. . . .

DEPUTY (*to* NED): Please help me, please help me.

MOLLY: You got a problem, stop *coming* here. You think

you're *filthy*, you think you're a *swine*, all those names you say while we're doing it. . . .

DEPUTY: I'm going to be sick.

MOLLY: You be sick, you be sick somewhere else.

The DEPUTY *runs out of the room. Beat.*

NED (*sighs*): Well . . .

MOLLY: He's got no cause to be coming here like that.

Beat.

NED: You don't like the guy what'd you go to bed with him for?

MOLLY: For fi' dollars. 'N' you got fi' dollars I'll go to bed with you, too. You think that's a sin? You think I care . . . ? Your mumbo jumbo. You think I care . . . ? I slep's with him, yeah, I'll sleep with anybody comes up the five bucks. That's evil? Throw me out, what you priests pay me to work here. Do your own goddamn washing. Don't you talk to *me* about God; don't you tell *me* about sin. Hey? Your religion is so good, your God, get Him to cure my little girl. Hey? Cure that girl out there. . . . Your blessed Shrine, your St. Ann. Eh? Your Weeping Virgin . . . ? Cure my little girl . . . get outta here . . . you got your nerve. . . .

NED: I . . .

MOLLY: I need a *man*, I need a *husband*, my little girl needs *help*, I got *nothing* . . . you gonna give me those things . . . ? (*Beat.*) You gonna give me those things?

Beat. MOLLY *finishes washing up. She turns her back to* NED, *puts her hair up in the yellow ribbon.* NED *recognizes her as the naked girl he saw through the window in the morning.*

NED: I wish I could.

MOLLY: I wish you could, too, but you *can't.* So whyn't you get the hell out of my room?

139   *Exterior: Shantytown—Molly's House—Day.*

Beat. NED *looks at her, leaves the room. CAMERA FOL-LOWS him out to the landing. He looks at the* LITTLE GIRL; *she looks at him.* NED *starts down the stairs.*

We see MOLLY *in the window doing something to her hair in the mirror. She calls the* LITTLE GIRL *to her; she puts on her shawl.* NED *comes out of the building, stands with his back to the CAMERA, looking up at* MOLLY.

140   *Angle:* NED *puts his hand in his pocket, turns it out.*

141   *Insert: His pocket is empty, except for two of the Shrine key chains.*

142   *Angle:* NED *looks back up at* MOLLY *longingly, sighs. A* TOWNSWOMAN *comes past.*

TOWNSWOMAN: Father, here . . .

She presses something into his hand. NED *looks at it.*

NED: What's this for?

TOWNSWOMAN (*walking on*): It's for your beautiful project.

NED *looks uncomprehendingly at her.*

TOWNSWOMAN: It's for the restoration of the Shrine.

NED: God bless you, I can't thank you enough.

TOWNSWOMAN: It's for a good cause.

NED: You don't know the half of it. (*He hurries after her.*) Here . . . (*He presses a key chain into her hand.*) Have a key chain. . . .

TOWNSWOMAN: Thank you.

She hurries on. NED *looks at the money she has given him.*

143   *Insert: His hand holding a five-dollar bill.*

144   *Angle:* NED *smiles, kisses the bill. He starts back toward the stairs to Molly's house. As he gets there,* MOLLY *comes out, leading her* LITTLE GIRL. MOLLY *carries her basket of laundry.*

NED: Actually, I've got five dollars *myself;* what do you say we . . .

She brushes past him.

MOLLY: Get out of my way. I've had enough of your bullshit for one day. I've got work to do.

145   *Interior: Monastery Cell—Day.*

        JIM *pacing back and forth, the SOUND of clanking. Swinging a censer. The incense is mounting in the room. He walks to the window, looks down.*

146   *Exterior: Monastery—Day.*

        Point of View: In the courtyard.

The SHERIFF, *a deputy, and the bloodhounds, quartering the area. We hear the* SOUND *of a knock on his door.*

147   *Angle:* JIM *turns to go to the door.*

JIM: Yeah, who is it . . . ?

YOUNG MONK (*offscreen*): Father . . . ?

JIM *opens the door. The* YOUNG MONK *is there.* JIM *puts down the censer. Beat.*

JIM: Yeah . . . ? What is it . . . ?

YOUNG MONK: I wanted to ask you . . . *A New Look at Deuteronomy.* You approach ten: nineteen. "Love the stranger, for you yourselves were strangers in the Land of Egypt," and you use the word a "sacrament."

JIM: You like that, huh?

YOUNG MONK: Yes, I appreciated it, and what I believed was an echo of the gnostic, the ecstatic *mode*, that is to say, a *true*, that is to say, a noninterpretive, understanding of the text.

Pause.

JIM: You *got* it!

YOUNG MONK: I *thought* that I did! Oh, forgive me if I'm running on, you know, here at the monastery, we're enjoined to silence most of the year. . . .

JIM: Yeah? What do you do?

YOUNG MONK: Pray . . . And it's such a pleasure, when the bonds are lifted, for the Feast of the Shrine, and then for this

week, all this *company*, and then, to have you and Father Riley
here . . .

JIM: Yeah, it's a heady thing. . . .

YOUNG MONK: And then we learned your *bags* were stolen,
and in line with that verse . . . kindness to the stranger, I
wanted you to have this.

The YOUNG MONK *gives him his rosary.*

JIM (*touched*): Gedouddahere . . .

YOUNG MONK: No. It's an honor. It's an honor meeting you.

JIM: Back at ya. Hey, thanks.

YOUNG MONK: Well . . .

The YOUNG MONK *bows himself out of the room.*

148   *Interior: The Refectory—Day.*

    The YOUNG MONK *opens the judas door, peeks back in
    at* JIM.

149   *Interior: Monastery Cell—Day.*

    Point of View: JIM *in the room, looks out the window, starts
    swinging his censer quickly, muttering to himself.*

JIM: Oh, God . . . Oh, God . . .

150   *Interior: The Refectory—Day.*

    Angle: The YOUNG MONK *closes the door. To himself, rever-
    ently.*

YOUNG MONK: What piety . . .

He starts down the hall.

151   Interior: Monastery Cell—Day.

    NED *comes into the room.*

NED: Shut up. We gotta get out of here. . . . The sheriff's . . .

A KNOCK on the door; the YOUNG MONK *reenters. Beat.*

YOUNG MONK: I *really* wanted to ask you, would you sign my book . . . ?

JIM: Yeah, sure, give it to me.

The YOUNG MONK *hands* JIM *the book* A New Look at Deuteronomy.

152   Insert: The book. JIM *signing it: "Good luck."*

YOUNG MONK (*offscreen*): We all especially enjoy your section about the Shrine.

JIM (*offscreen*): You like that, huh . . . ?

YOUNG MONK (*offscreen*): Very much.

153   Angle: The three of them, JIM *signing.*

JIM (*to* NED, *sotto*): Which one am I?

NED (*to* YOUNG MONK): I think Father Brown and I have to talk.

JIM *signs the book. The* YOUNG MONK *turns the book over.*

154   Insert: The inscription reads, "Good luck, Brown and

*Riley." The book is turned over again, to the back-cover
photo, showing the two heavy men, one in a cowboy hat.*

155   *Angle: The* YOUNG MONK *looking up at* JIM *and* NED.

YOUNG MONK: This photo doesn't do you justice.

JIM: Where *can* you find justice in this world?

155A   *Interior: Monastery—Refectory—Day.*

> *The* YOUNG MONK *nods reflectively.* NED *takes* JIM *by the
> arm, and they proceed out into the refectory. The* YOUNG
> MONK *follows, and the CAMERA FOLLOWS.*

YOUNG MONK: You'll be coming in the Procession tomorrow?

NED: Depends on how things fall out. I can't give you a
definite yes or no . . . if you'd excuse us, please . . . we have to
talk about *writing* things.

YOUNG MONK: Of *course.*

The YOUNG MONK *nods respectfully. CAMERA FOLLOWS* NED
and JIM *for a beat.*

156   *Interior: Chapel—Day.*

> *One old* FAT MONK *praying,* NED *and* JIM *come into the
> church, look around.* NED *slips the clippers out from the
> pew, and the two of them go into the confessional.*

157   *Interior: Confessional—Day.*

JIM: What took you so long?

NED: I got busy.

JIM: That kid gave me his beads.

NED: I'm very happy for you. Hold still.

NED *gets the clippers on him; we hear the chain POP.*

JIM: Oh, *thank* you.

NED: Now, a dash across the river, and it's Free Street, baby.

JIM: I'm with you, Neddy.

NED: Some booze and some broads and this country can kiss my ass.

They start out of the confessional.

158   *Interior: Monastery—Chapel—Day.*

The FAT MONK *looks up as the two come out of the confessional box. Beat.* NED *and* JIM *look at the* FAT MONK. *The* FAT MONK *looks at them questioningly. Beat.* NED *and* JIM *run out of the church.*

159   *Exterior: Monastery—Day.*

CAMERA FOLLOWS *them PAST the conference we have seen earlier, various priests disputing.*

FATHER LEVESQUE: Ah! Father Brown, Father Riley, perhaps you could settle an abstruse point for us . . .

NED (*shrugs*): I never got the knack of it.

They keep walking.

FATHER LEVESQUE (*calling after them*): We'll see you tonight at the Shrine? Do you have a request for the Procession?

160   Exterior: Shantytown—Day.

NED *and* JIM *hurrying toward the border.*

JIM: What is this thing with the Shrine?

NED: Some Shrine, it's some Madonna, it cries, it works miracles.

JIM: It what, it what, it changes things into other things . . . ?

NED: I don't know.

CAMERA FOLLOWS them THROUGH the short main street of the town, TOWARD the border.

NED: We hit the border, you make the sign of the cross over the guy, I make the sign of the cross over the guy. (*He hands him a Bible.*) Mumble something, look down in your book, here we go. . . .

CAMERA FOLLOWS them PAST the wanted poster of the three convicts. JIM *turns to look at the poster. He hunches down into his coat, pulls the muffler up over his face.* NED *combs his hair down over his forehead.*

JIM: What do you think happened to Bobby . . . ?

NED: I don't know. I hope he made it, too.

JIM: What's the first thing you're going to do when you get free, Ned?

NED: Keep your mouth off it, Jim, and we'll talk about it on the northern side.

160A   Exterior: Town Square—Day.

> *They pass under the banner which reads,* RESTORE THE SHRINE OF ST. ANN. *They pass the hardware store owner.*

SHOPKEEPER: Afternoon, Father . . .

They both nod to him. CAMERA CONTINUES as the two progress toward the border.

JIM: I'm gonna do, I'm gonna do, I'm gonna do something *important.*

NED: Yeah, that's fine.

JIM: I figure you're only alive so long, you might as well *do* something with yourself.

NED: Uh-huh.

They continue toward the border, where a GUARD *is processing a line of people. He recognizes them from a distance and waves. They wave back.*

NED: Piece of cake. Head in the book, read the book, mumble, over we go.

161   Exterior: Town Square—Day.

Angle: In the background, the warden's boat can be seen chugging down the river. Dark figures silhouetted on it, dogs straining on leashes. NED *and* JIM *move forward. We hear a man's VOICE: "Hold on one minute. . . ."* NED *and* JIM *look up. It is the* DEPUTY. *He comes over.*

DEPUTY: I just wanted to thank you.

NED: Hey, you don't owe me anything. . . . Glad to do it. Glad to be of a chance to help.

NED *looks around. Sotto ("Oh, no . . .")*

JIM *(sotto):* What?

NED *(inclines his head, sotto):* It's the warden.

162   *Point of View: The warden's boat—Day. Through the mist, chugging relentlessly toward them. Prominent on it a heavyset man in an impresario coat. He carries a riding crop, whips the dogs to silence them.*

162A   *Exterior: Warden's Boat—Dusk.*

WARDEN *Point of view of town.*

163   *Exterior: Town Square—Day.*

Close-up: JIM *frightened.*

DEPUTY *(offscreen):* It's so rare that someone *cares,* you know, or that you didn't say I was weak, or . . .

164   Angle: The warden's boat reaching the Canadian shore. The dogs leap into the water, dragging the guards with them. JIM is very frightened, starts to rub his back.

NED: Don't even speak about it, really.

DEPUTY: And I think I'm gonna tell my wife, just put it all at her feet.

NED: That's a great idea.

DEPUTY: And I just wanted to thank you. . . . (*Beat.*) Can you shake hands with a priest?

NED: I don't know why not. . . .

They shake hands.

DEPUTY: Thank you.

NED: You're very . . . very . . . (*Hands the* DEPUTY *a Shrine key chain.*) Keep on the bright side!

He makes the sign of the cross to wave the man away. The DEPUTY *moves away. The* WARDEN *and his prison officials in uniform move up toward the bridge. They are met by the* SHERIFF. *With the* WARDEN *and the* SHERIFF *in the background,* JIM *starts to push toward the border.*

NED: Don't run, don't run. We're okay. Don't run. It's okay.

The group with the WARDEN *and* NED *and* JIM *converge on the border from two different directions.* NED *and* JIM *get behind a short line of people being examined.*

165   *Close-up:* NED *and* JIM.

NED *(sotto):* It's okay. One more minute and over we go.

JIM *(sotto):* I can't go back in the joint.

NED: You don't *have* to. Just read the book.

NED *looks back surreptitiously at the* WARDEN *and the* SHERIFF.

166   *Exterior: Canadian Customs/Border—Day.*

> *Point of View: The group with the* WARDEN *coming closer.*
> *HOLD.*

167   *Exterior: U.S. Customs/Border—Day.*

> *Close-up:* NED.

> *He is sweating, very nervous.*

BORDER GUARD *(offscreen):* Father, Father, you can come up here.

168   *Angle: The line at the border.* NED *and* JIM *fourth and fifth in the line. The* BORDER GUARD *is speaking to them.*

BORDER GUARD: Gentlemen, it's all right. Folks, let 'em pass, please.

The two convicts move to the front of the line.

BORDER GUARD: Looking forward to the Procession.

NED *and* JIM, *anxious, right at the border.*

NED: Aren't we all.

BORDER GUARD (*pointing to the* DEPUTY): Friend tells me you folks are the authors of some pretty deep books.

NED: Well, you know, depends on your taste.

BORDER GUARD: Like to *read* 'em, if I could, I think of myself as a good Catholic.

NED: We'll *send* you some.

BORDER GUARD: Yep. Did a little writing *myself,* once.

NED: *Did* you, now.

BORDER GUARD: No luck *selling* it, though, I don't suppose you'd . . .

NED: Oh, my goodness . . . did we say our silent prayer . . . ?

JIM *shakes his head no.*

NED (*to* BORDER GUARD): . . . little busy right now . . .

BORDER GUARD: Yes, I understand . . . God bless . . .

He waves them through. NED *looks back over his shoulder.*

169   *Exterior: Canadian Customs/Border—Day.*

> *Point of View: The* SHERIFF, *the* WARDEN, *and the prison guards. The* WARDEN *holds up three gold coins.*

WARDEN: . . . instruct my men to shoot on sight, or at my command. *One hundred dollars* on the head of each man. *Dead.*

SHERIFF: Um-hum . . .

WARDEN: . . . one hundred dollars—*gold.*

SHERIFF: Well, you give us the *sign.* . . .

170   *Exterior: Bridge—Day.*

    Angle: NED *and* JIM *start across the bridge. We hear:*

MOLLY (*offscreen*): You didn't answer my *question* . . . ? Father? Father?

171   *Exterior: Bridge—Day.*

    Angle: MOLLY *carrying a basket of laundry, her* LITTLE GIRL *behind her, stopping the two.*

MOLLY: You didn't answer my question. Is your Shrine going to cure my little girl . . . ? You told me to be true. I thought about it, and I thought I *would* be true. I'd be *glad* to be true. What's in it for *me?* You understand? If I "believe . . ."?

NED: I can't talk to you now.

MOLLY: Well, you could talk to me *before,* when all you had was "shame" and all. Why can't you talk "now"? Why can't you talk "now"?

NED: You're making a scene. . . .

MOLLY: What's that compared to eternal life . . . ?

NED: Yeah, you got a lot of spunk, now just get out of here, will ya, babe . . . ?

MOLLY: Screw *you*, Your Holiness. You think I didn't see the way you looked at me, I said that I'd go to *bed* with you . . . ?

NED (*sotto*): Will you for chrissakes shut up?

MOLLY: What are you, too scared or too cheap! If God *really* made the world, he should of put some *men* in it. . . .

NED *looks at the* WARDEN.

172   Point of View: The WARDEN *talking to the* SHERIFF.

WARDEN: . . . got to be in this area, or they would have frozen in the woods. We've got the bridge locked up, tonight we go house to house, all the residents, bring out anybody who's a stranger. Weather's on our side. We'll find 'em. . . .

MOLLY (*offscreen*): You want to answer my question, Father . . . ?

173   Angle: NED *draws* MOLLY *aside.* JIM *follows. The line moves up. CAMERA MOVES IN on the group of* NED, MOLLY, *and* JIM.

NED: I can't talk to you now.

MOLLY: You want to lead us to the Shrine, and wash away our sins? *I'm* ready to change. . . .

NED *looks over his shoulder. The* WARDEN *and the* SHERIFF *have taken up positions at the bridge.*

174   Close-up: NED. *He sighs.*

175   Angle: NED *and* JIM *dejected.*

NED (*softly*): Damn you.

MOLLY: I'm already damned, Father, I'm damned to hell for adultery. I'm damned for eternity. What's a little rudeness going to get me? Two more weeks . . . ?

She starts away down the street with her washing, followed by her LITTLE GIRL. NED *and* JIM *walking at her side.*

176   Close-up: NED *and* JIM.

MOLLY (*offscreen*): That's what *I* want to know. Everybody's saying, how I got to live my life. *Eat* first, that's what I say. Eat first, then talk about what's right and wrong.

JIM *looks back over his shoulder.*

177   Point of View: The border. The SHERIFF *and the* WARDEN *screening the travelers.*

WARDEN: Well, if they're down here, let's *find* 'em. I say a house-to-house search.

178   Exterior: Town Square—Dusk.

Angle: NED *and* JIM *retreating,* MOLLY *following.*

MOLLY: Eat first, and then talk about what's a crime. You had no business to come to my room. Is that the act of a man . . . ?

179   Angle: The group stop by the gazebo.

NED: Hey, hey, who are *you*? *You* don't know what my life is. Whyn't you live for yourself? Whyn't you go live your own life . . . ?

MOLLY: Why don't *you*? Who the hell are you to talk to me? Why are you stuck up in a *monastery*? Watch my little girl.

MOLLY *takes her basket of washing and mounts the steps to the house, leaving* JIM *and* NED *alone with the* GIRL. *Beat.* NED *looks back toward the bridge.*

180   Exterior: Bridge—Dusk.

> *Point of View: The* WARDEN, *berating the* SHERIFF *on the bridge.*

WARDEN: Every house. Clear it out, send the *dogs* in . . . smoke 'em out. . . .

SHERIFF: Well, people *live* here.

WARDEN: I don't give a goddamn, they can live here when those men are dead.

181   Exterior: Town Square—Gazebo—Dusk.

> *Angle:* NED *and* JIM *with the* LITTLE GIRL.

NED: All right . . . how do we get past the warden?

JIM *motions "not in front of the little girl."*

NED: She's deaf.

JIM *looks down at her.*

182   *Angle: The* LITTLE GIRL.

NED (*offscreen*): Okay, okay. We can do this. We can do this. We need a little thought.

183   *Angle:* JIM *and the* LITTLE GIRL. *He caresses her head; she looks up.*

NED (*offscreen*): We need a *plan* and we're not going to panic.

184   *Angle: The* LITTLE GIRL *looks up at* JIM, *behind whom is a poster of the convicts.*

185   *Exterior: Town Square/Bridge—Dusk* (*starts snowing*).

Angle: The bridge. The WARDEN *walking down toward them; with him militiamen and dogs, the* SHERIFF *following.*

SHERIFF: We have a populace.

WARDEN: You don't have a populace, Sheriff. When I'm gone, you have a populace. All you have now is a bunch of suspects.

SHERIFF: All I'm saying now is go easy.

WARDEN: Easy? You've got the wrong man.

186   *Angle: The two convicts. They look from the approaching* WARDEN *to the house.* MOLLY *is coming down the steps.* NED *and* JIM *start down the street, away from the* WARDEN. *The* LITTLE GIRL *looks after them.*

187   *Exterior: Town Street—Dusk.*

Angle: NED *and* JIM *walk in the street. It is starting to snow heavily.*

NED: We've been in tougher spots than this before.

JIM *looks behind him.*

188   *Exterior: Town Square—Dusk (snowing).*

Angle: The WARDEN, SHERIFF, *militiamen, and dogs, fanning out.*

WARDEN: Let's start right here 'n' work down the hill.

SHERIFF: Here? Warden, there's nobody here but the monks.

WARDEN: Yes? Well, why don't we make *sure* . . . ?

189   *Exterior: Blacksmith Shop—Night (snowing).*

Angle: JIM *steers* NED *off a side street, quickly.* JIM *looks down, panting, trying to catch his breath.*

JIM: Uh-ho . . .

190   *Point of View: The ground—Night (snowing). On the ground in the tracks in the snow, imprinted by the soles of their shoes, we read, "Property of the State Prison System."*

191   *Angle:* JIM *and* NED *take off their shoes, start to walk on the cold earth. As they hurry down the street, they meet the* YOUNG MONK. *The* YOUNG MONK *shows them the clothespin he wears on his neck.*

YOUNG MONK: Good luck on the lottery tonight.

JIM: Uh-huh.

YOUNG MONK: The drawing's after vespers. It's a long shot, but "You never know."

JIM: Yeah, that's the truth.

They look back.

192   *Exterior: Town Square—Night (snowing).*

    Point of View: A deputy holding the bloodhounds, rounding the corner. The bloodhounds sniffing.

193   *Exterior: Monastery—Night (snowing).*

    Angle: JIM *and* NED *mount the steps of the monastery.*

YOUNG MONK: You aren't wearing your shoes.

JIM: It brings us closer to the earth.

JIM *and* NED *look around, then enter the building. The* YOUNG MONK *shakes his head in admiration and bends down, begins to remove his shoes.*

194   *Interior: Monastery Chapel—Night.*

    The two in the darkened church, trying to catch their breath. The two look around.

195   *Point of View: Panorama of the church interior. It STOPS on the Shrine of the Madonna.*

196   *Angle: The two convicts look up at the Shrine.*

JIM: This is the statue that cries.

NED: I guess it is.

JIM: And what does it do? It grants wishes.

NED: Hmmm.

JIM: I know what I'd wish for, right now, I'd wish for two new pairs of shoes.

We hear the SOUND of a door opening. The two cower, move behind a pillar.

197   *Point of View: A sliding door into a robing room. A monk leaving the robing room with piles of vestments; beyond, shelves full of clothes.*

198   *Interior: Robing Room—Night.*

   Angle: The two convicts shrug, move into the robing room. They find a rack of shoes. They sit, start trying on the shoes. Beat.

JIM: I say we try the river tonight, Ned.

NED: What do we do, walk on the water?

JIM: Steal a boat . . . ?

NED: They got the waterfront sewed tighter than a football.

JIM: Hell, whaddaya, whaddaya, Neddy. We're not going back. Bob, *Bobby* got across. . . .

NED: We don't know that he got across.

JIM: We got to believe that, Ned. We got to.

NED: We do?

JIM: Yeah.

NED: Why?

Beat.

JIM: Because if we don't, what will we believe . . . ?

We hear the SOUNDS of the WARDEN shouting commands to his men. NED goes to the window. Looks out.

199   *Exterior: Town Street—Night.*

   Point of View: The WARDEN, dogs, and men.

WARDEN: You got the convicts' clothing? We're going house to house 'n' we're starting *here*. Get the dogs.

200   *Interior: Robing Room—Night.*

   NED shakes his head sadly. SOUND of bells. He looks back at JIM, who is at the door, about to leave.

NED: Where are you going?

JIM: I'm going to prayers and dinner.

Beat. NED nods. JIM exits. NED is alone for a moment. He sighs. He starts out of the robing room.

201   *Point of View: The Madonna looking down.*

202   *Angle: NED looks at the Madonna, looks out the window.*

203   *Exterior: Town Street—Night (snowing).*

Point of View: The WARDEN *and deputies and dogs going door to door.*

204   *Interior: Monastery—Chapel—Night.*

Angle: NED *at the foot of the statue, looks up.*

NED (*very softly*): I never thought I'm such a bad man. (*Pause.*) If I've been wrong, I'm sorry. (*Pause.*) *Please* don't let them take me back. . . .

He hangs his head. Beat. We hear the SOUND of a raindrop. Beat. ANOTHER. NED *holds out his palm. Raindrops fall slowly in his palm.* NED *looks up.*

205   *Point of View: The Madonna's face. She is crying. Offscreen: the BARK of dogs, growing louder.*

206   *Close-up:* NED *looking at the Madonna. Beat. Offscreen: BARKING DOGS.*

FATHER LEVESQUE (*offscreen*): And, of course, it's just a hole in the roof.

207   *Angle:* NED *looks around, at* FATHER LEVESQUE, *who is standing in front of the statue, a large fat cat in his arms.*

NED: Hello, Father.

FATHER LEVESQUE: That's the wonderful thing about what you have written, you and your friend. (*Beat.*) That we never forget that it's simply a hole in the roof.

FATHER LEVESQUE *and then* NED *look up.*

208   *Point of View: The hole in the roof—Night. The water dripping on the head of the Madonna.*

FATHER LEVESQUE (*offscreen*): That's why we were so glad that you could come.

209   *Angle:* FATHER LEVESQUE *and* NED. *The SOUND of dogs barking, growing louder. The cat leaps from* FATHER LE- VESQUE's *arms and darts down the aisle.* NED *watches it go.*

FATHER LEVESQUE: Your notion of the real meaning of a miracle. Well . . . (*He starts to move off.*) I just wanted to thank you. . . . I'm sorry if I disturbed you.

210   *Exterior: Monastery—Night (snowing).*

    The cat darts across the snow. The dogs howl and follow, dragging the deputies with them.

211   *Interior: Monastery—Chapel—Night.*

NED: Uh-huh, yeah, I was just . . .

Beat.

FATHER LEVESQUE (*smiling*): The word you're looking for is "praying," I believe.

Beat. FATHER LEVESQUE *comes over and puts his arm on* NED's *shoulders.*

FATHER LEVESQUE: It's not easy to be a priest. Yes. I know. (*Beat.*) It's all right, my son.

NED: Sometimes . . .

FATHER LEVESQUE (*nodding*): Yes.

NED: Sometimes you just need *help.*

FATHER LEVESQUE: Yes.

NED: . . . and there *is* no help.

FATHER LEVESQUE: Did you ask *her*?

NED: I suppose I *did*.

FATHER LEVESQUE: For what?

NED: For help to get from one place to another.

FATHER LEVESQUE: *Well* . . .

He makes the sign of the cross, starts to move off.

FATHER LEVESQUE: . . . Will you be marching in the Procession tomorrow . . . ?

NED (*sighs*): No, Father . . . (*Pause.*) In truth, I have other things to do.

FATHER LEVESQUE: I understand. (*Smiles.*) And it's a long walk into Canada.

Beat.

NED: Into Canada . . . ?

FATHER LEVESQUE: It's a long walk all the way with the Shrine, into Canada.

NED: Oh, are we still doing that?

FATHER LEVESQUE: What?

NED: Carrying it, the, into Canada . . . ?

FATHER LEVESQUE (*laughs*): Well, yes, that's right. We're still doing it! Right across the bridge, and to our sister church, on the Canadian side.

FATHER LEVESQUE *moves off.* NED *looks up at the Madonna.*

212   *Point of View: The face of the Madonna, a very slight smile on her face.*

213   *Exterior: Monastery—Day.*

       JIM *comes out of the church, looks around.*

214   *Exterior: Sawmill—Day.*

       The lumber mill carriage shed of the church. The monks are building the finishing touches on the effigy of the Virgin, which will, when Bob gets shot, be the thing where Jim goes to steal the dollar bills, and, again, in which Bob will hide. The effigy should be large, about ten feet tall, and should have a niche in it in which the actual *Weeping Virgin should be placed. The SOUND of hammering, a float being constructed in the background. A* MONK *comes into the FRAME.*

MONK: Excuse me, Father.

215   *Angle:* JIM *sits on a pile of planks, looking out over the river. The* MONK *asking him to move.* JIM *shifts over; CAMERA FOLLOWS him. He moves to one side, starts to sit down. Sees something off to his side . . . the wanted poster.* JIM *moves again.*

       CAMERA FOLLOWS him outside, where he sits on a fence.

216   *Point of View: The far side of the river.*

217   *Angle:* JIM *sitting, looking; the SOUND of hammering. He flinches with each stroke of the hammer. He gingerly touches his back.*

JIM (*sotto*): I gotta get over to the other side.

YOUNG MONK: Surely it's not time yet. . . .

JIM *turns, uncomprehending.*

YOUNG MONK: Father? Surely it's not up to us when we go?

JIM *looks at him for a moment. Beat.*

JIM: You ever been helpless?

Pause.

YOUNG MONK: Certainly.

JIM: Whaddaya do about it?

Pause.

YOUNG MONK: Pray.

218   JIM *thinks about this for a moment.*

219   *Interior: Monastery—Refectory—Day.*

> *The staging area for the Procession, people bustling about, the banner overhead,* CELEBRATE THE PROCESSION OF ST. ANN. NED, *asking directions of a monk, is directed toward what is obviously the command post of the procession. He walks;* CAMERA FOLLOWS. *Behind a large table are seated* FATHER NOGULICH, *the Yugoslav priest, and his* TRANSLATOR. *Priests are bringing the Yugoslav priest garments to okay, forms to sign; the two are very busy.* NED *comes up; all his remarks are translated to, and then translated from, Yugoslavian by the* TRANSLATOR.

NED: I changed my mind, I wanna march in the Procession.

TRANSLATOR: Too late.

NED: What do you mean, "too late . . ."?

TRANSLATOR: You're late, you're a day late.

NED: We got delayed.

TRANSLATOR (*shrugs*): We have, we've just closed up the list. . . .

He holds up the list; the TRANSLATOR *and* FATHER NOGULICH *shrug, after the manner of bureaucrats everywhere.*

NED: Well, open the list up.

TRANSLATOR: Can't do it.

NED: Uh-huh, uh-huh . . . you want me to go above your head?

The TRANSLATOR *and* FATHER NOGULICH *confer.*

TRANSLATOR: We do not understand the meaning of the phrase.

NED: It means I'm going to go to the head man and puke all over ya, I got a *problem,* and I got a right to march in the *Procession* . . . now, you sign me up.

TRANSLATOR: This is not a Christian attitude.

NED: *Tough.*

The TRANSLATOR *and* FATHER NOGULICH *confer. Beat.*

TRANSLATOR: He says that there is something "wrong" about you.

NED: You tell him that he don't know the *half* of it, unless he puts my *name* on that list.

Beat. FATHER NOGULICH *looks long and hard at* NED, *who returns the stare. Beat.* FATHER NOGULICH *nods to the* TRANSLA- TOR, *who signs the list.*

TRANSLATOR (*softly*): All right . . .

NED *turns to go.*

TRANSLATOR: And who will your afflicted be . . . ?

Beat. NED *stops, turns back.*

NED: I'm sorry . . . ?

TRANSLATOR: Are you deaf, who will your afflicted be . . . ?

NED: . . . afflicted . . . ?

TRANSLATOR (*petulantly*): Who will you be escorting?

NED: . . . escorting . . . ?

TRANSLATOR (*as if to a child*): Who will be the afflicted per- son you will be escorting in prayer, for the intercession of the Virgin?

NED: Uh, we thought that we'd just go ourselves. . . .

The TRANSLATOR *throws up his hands, as does* FATHER NOGULICH.

TRANSLATOR: Yes, yes, that's *lovely* . . . let's live our lives with no rules at all . . . ! (*He taps his list with the pen.*) Who will be the afflicted person you will be escorting across . . . ?

220   *Exterior: Monastery—Day.*

NED, *looking for something; CAMERA FOLLOWS him down the street. The workmen are bringing out the effigy, and a couple of townspeople come over to it and start pinning money to it. He sees the* LITTLE GIRL; *he hurries up to her.*

NED: Where's your mother? (*He remembers she can't speak.*) Aaah . . .

He looks around.

221   *Exterior: Shantytown—Molly's House—Day.*

Point of View: MOLLY *coming out of her house with her basket of laundry.*

222   *Angle:* NED *goes over to her; he tries to take the laundry from her. She resists. She walks on;* NED *and the* CAMERA MOVE *with her.*

MOLLY: Ah, Mr. Holiness, no, I don't need your help.

NED: I want to *ask* you something.

MOLLY: What, do I want to go upstairs for a *ride* . . . ? You know, you got a lot of nerve. . . .

NED: Yeah, I'm a sinner. . . .

MOLLY: Big of you to *say* so.

NED: But I want to *change.* . . .

MOLLY: Good luck.

NED: I think it's time to make a gesture.

MOLLY: Go make it.

NED: I want to take your little girl in the Procession of the *Shrine*.

Beat.

MOLLY: You go to hell.

Beat.

NED: What's the matter, don't you believe in divine grace . . . ?

MOLLY: I *told* you: Piss off. You take your carnival and shake down someone *else*.

NED: If God . . .

MOLLY *stops, turns to him.*

MOLLY: I *told* you: *I don't need your magic show.* I don't want your goddamn mumbo jumbo, 'n' I won't curse my *kid* with it. You *got* it . . . ?

NED (*He takes her arm; stops her*): Please. Please. (*Beat.*) Please, isn't there anything . . . isn't there *anything* which would change your mind . . . ? *What* could I do to change your mind . . . ?

Beat.

MOLLY (*reflectively*): Uh-huh . . . (*Beat.*) I'll tell you what would convince me. . . .

NED: What?

Beat.

MOLLY: What's the most important thing in the world . . . ?

223 *Interior: Monastery—Day.*

JIM *and the* YOUNG MONK *proceeding in a stately fashion down the hall.*

JIM: And what about all this no talking stuff . . . ?

YOUNG MONK: Well, as you know, our order subscribes to the Rule of Silence. . . .

JIM: . . . uh-huh . . .

YOUNG MONK: . . . except for the few days of the *Procession.*

JIM: Uh-huh, and, is that no talking stuff, is that *hard* . . . ?

YOUNG MONK: Actually, *no,* I think it's quite *refreshing.* . . .

JIM *nods.*

YOUNG MONK: And, I believe, you've written *yourself,* if you recall what I'm *speaking* of in Deuteronomy . . . four: twelve . . . ?

JIM: Four: twelve.

YOUNG MONK: "Ye heard the voice of the words . . ."?

JIM: Oh. In four: *twelve,* yeah . . .

NED (*offscreen*): Jimmy!

The YOUNG MONK *and* JIM *turn.*

224   Angle: NED *coming hurriedly down the hall, catches up to the two.*

JIM: Hiya, Ned.

The YOUNG MONK *nods. Beat. The* YOUNG MONK *indicates they should proceed.* NED *follows.*

JIM (*to* YOUNG MONK): Well, is there anything *else* I should . . . oh, oh oh . . . ?

He fingers the rough cloth of the monk's habit.

JIM: Is this stuff scratchy?

YOUNG MONK: You get used to it.

NED (*sotto*): Jimmy, I got to talk to you.

JIM: Not now, Ned.

NED: Jimmy . . .

JIM: I got it whipt, okay, I made my mind up.

NED: What, what?

They have arrived at a massive oaken door. The YOUNG MONK *KNOCKS solemnly.*

JIM: I'm gonna check into the *deal* here.

NED: What deal?

YOUNG MONK (*proudly*): Father Brown is going to join our order.

NED (*to Jim*): You're *what?*

JIM (*sotto*): Hey, it's three squares and a cot.

NED *and* JIM *have a whispered exchange.*

NED: *Jimmy* . . .

JIM: I tol' you I'm not going back there, Ned.

NED: I got the way out . . . Jim. I got the way *out.* . . .

The YOUNG MONK *KNOCKS on the door again.*

JIM: You do . . . ?

NED: Yeah.

A large VOICE is heard from behind the oak door.

FATHER LEVESQUE (*offscreen*): Enter.

The YOUNG MONK *swings open the oak door. He looks to* JIM. *Beat.*

NED (*to Jim; sotto*): You're 'bout three hundred feet from freedom, Jimmy. I can get us across. Don't go native on me here. (*To* YOUNG MONK.) Whaddaya trying to do, shanghai my pal . . . ?

NED *leans into the room beyond the oak door. To the scene beyond.*

NED: Changed our mind. Changed our minds. Sorry.

He swings the door shut, starts walking away with JIM. *CAMERA FOLLOWS them.* JIMMY *looks back over his shoulder at the* YOUNG MONK, *shrugs.*

JIM: I can't believe it, Ned, they're gonna catch us.

NED: No, I *promise* you, no. All we need is a hundred bucks from that Shrine out there.

The two confer.

NED *gestures with his head; both turn their heads.*

225   *Exterior: Monastery—Day.*

> *Point of View: Out the window. The banner reading,* CON-
> TRIBUTE TO RESTORE THE SHRINE OF ST. ANN. *Below the
> banner is the effigy, now getting fairly well covered with bills
> the passersby are pinning to it.*

226   *Interior/Exterior: Monastery—Day.*

> NED *and* JIM *walking. They walk past a small conference of
> priests. One* PRIEST *is speaking and gesturing to a drawing
> of the Madonna. His remarks are rendered into English by a*
> TRANSLATOR. *The* PRIEST *speaks in Serbo-Croatian; the*
> TRANSLATOR *translates.*

TRANSLATOR: The Albigensian heresy, at which time Cardinal Archbishop Frotti was asked to take action on the issue
of, as it was termed then, Mariolatry, and . . . ah, Father
Brown, Father Riley.

227   *Angle:* NED *and* JIM *stop.*

TRANSLATOR: Since you've written on this so well, will *you* tell
us what Cardinal Archbishop Frotti did . . . ?

Beat.

JIM: Hey, what would *you* have done?

The assemblage nods and sighs in complete agreement. The
TRANSLATOR *translates for the Yugoslav* PRIEST, *who also nods*

his agreement. NED *and* JIM *continue down the hall.* NED *looks over at the effigy outside.* JIM *turns to look.*

228   *Exterior: Town Street—Day.*

> *Point of View: The effigy. The effigy moves slowly toward the town square. The* YOUNG MONK *comes INTO the FRAME, looking after* JIM *and* NED. *He sighs softly.*

229   *Exterior: Monastery—Day.*

> NED *and* JIM *proceed toward the effigy. The* TRANSLATOR *is holding a clipboard.*

TRANSLATOR: And let's make sure that we perform it right.

NED: We're gonna be fine, don't you worry.

TRANSLATOR: Let us see that we will be. When the Procession *starts (he hands Ned a mimeographed sheet)* I will be holding part of the float. Father Levesque will say, "Suffer the little children to come unto me ..." I will hold out my hand....

NED: *Okay,* okay ... fine ...

He gestures JIM *to go on.*

230   *Exterior: Town Square—Day.*

> *Angle:* JIM *moving stealthily toward the effigy. CAMERA MOVES with him. He looks around. Sidles closer to the effigy.* JIM *starts to move toward the effigy. Someone comes by.* JIM *retires. Beat. He tries to move toward it again. Two people come by. They nod.* JIM *nods. Sighs. Beat. Beat. The* SHOPKEEPER *comes past, tips his hat.*

SHOPKEEPER: Evening, Father.

JIM *nods. Beat. Looks after the* SHOPKEEPER, *who is walking away.*

231   Exterior: Monastery—Day.

> *Angle:* NED *still buttonholed by the* TRANSLATOR.

TRANSLATOR: And you say *what* . . . ?

NED *sighs, looks at his sheet, reads.*

NED: "Volo. I will pray for the intercession for this poor unfortunate."

TRANSLATOR: *Yes.* And *then* . . . ?

MOLLY (*offscreen*): You got my money . . . ?

NED *turns.*

232   Exterior: Monastery—Day.

> *Angle:* MOLLY *leading her* LITTLE GIRL *by the hand. The* LITTLE GIRL *dressed in a white, clean, but very ratty communion dress.* NED *and the* TRANSLATOR *turn to look at her. Beat.*

MOLLY: You got my money . . . ? The Procession's starting in fifteen minutes, and if you want . . .

NED, *shushing her, moves her away from the* TRANSLATOR.

NED: Yes, yes, *fine* . . .

CAMERA MOVES with them as NED *moves her around the side of the building.*

TRANSLATOR (*shouting after them*): And when we reach the middle of the bridge . . .

NED (*calling back to him*): It's going to be *fine, willya* . . . ?

233   *Angle:* NED *and* MOLLY.

MOLLY: You got my money?

NED: Hey, you are one *money-grubbing* bitch. . . .

He draws her aside, beneath the monastery struts.

MOLLY: *Whatever,* but the kid don't march in the parade, without I get a hundred bucks.

NED: You're gonna get your money, you're gonna *get* your goddamn money, how'd you *get* this way . . . ?

MOLLY: None of your business, what are you to me . . . ? What are you to me . . . ? *Nothing,* you want me to *pray,* you want me to *screw,* you want me to march in the parade . . . *pay* me.

NED: Hey, nice talk in front of your kid.

MOLLY: . . . she can't hear you, she's *deaf.* . . .

SOUND of a gunshot. NED *flinches. Another SHOT.* NED *hesitates, moves around the building, peers out.*

234   *Exterior: Town.*

   Point of View: The commotion in the street, birds flying. People running.

235   *Exterior: Monastery/Shantytown Boardwalk—Day.*

   Angle: NED *moves out past the side of the building. Calling.*

NED: What *is* it . . . ?

PASSERBY (*running*): They *shot* 'em.

NED: They shot who . . . ? *They shot who . . . ?*

The PASSERBY *running away, over his shoulder.*

PASSERBY: The one they were *lookin'* for, the convict. He was trying to steal the money . . . !

236   *Exterior: Town Square—Day.*

   Another PASSERBY *runs from the direction of the shooting.*

SECOND PASSERBY: They shot the convict!

NED (*softly*): Oh, hell . . . Jimmy. (*He looks around.*) Where, where . . . ?

SECOND PASSERBY: He ran in the hardware store.

THIRD PASSERBY: They chased him into the hardware store; he tried to get a gun.

237   *Exterior: Town Square—Day.*

   People running toward the SOUND of the shots. NED *running. He stops outside the general store, people milling about. Militiamen are being directed by the* SHERIFF. *The* WARDEN *pushes through the mob into the store.*

PASSERBY: Warden . . .

WARDEN: Lemme through.

The WARDEN *enters the store.*

NED (*to* BYSTANDER): What happened?

BYSTANDER: I don't know, they . . .

The WARDEN *comes out.*

WARDEN: Send for the doc. Get a couple men over here. . . .

BYSTANDER: Is that the . . .

WARDEN: Yep. It's him all right, we got our convict, no doubt about it . . .

WARDEN *goes back into the store. Two men come out supporting the* DEPUTY, *who has been slightly wounded.*

DEPUTY #2: Oh, Lord, Oh Lord, I'm *shot,* the man in there *shot* me. . . .

The DEPUTY *and his supporters pass.* NED *looks after them. Beat. He holds his gaze on something in the distance.*

238   *Point of View: The* DEPUTY *moving OUT OF THE FRAME, beyond him, the bridge, unguarded, as the militiamen and guards all race over toward the site of the shooting.*

BYSTANDER (*offscreen*): Yep. I think he's dying. Tried to *disguise* himself . . . knew they'd catch him.

239   *Close-up:* NED *rubs his forehead.*

BYSTANDER (*offscreen*): . . . how'd they ever think they could get away . . . somebody said "send for the doc," b' I bet they need a *priest.* . . .

NED *looks up to heaven for guidance. Beat.* NED *starts through the mob.*

NED (*sadly*): I'm a priest. . . .

239A   Interior: General Store/Hotel—Day.

> *The mob starts to part; CAMERA FOLLOWS* NED *into the store.*

BYSTANDERS (*offscreen*): Let 'em through . . . (*etc.*).

CAMERA FOLLOWS NED *into the store. Beyond him, on the far side of the store, is the* SHOPKEEPER, *who, very shaken, is talking to the* DEPUTY.

SHOPKEEPER: . . . tried to steal, I saw him near the *gun case*, and, and, and, I knew he was the man. . . .

240   Close-up: NED, *his face, pushing through the crowd.*

241   Point of View: The WARDEN *talking to a deputy.*

WARDEN: Get 'em outta here, and get 'em locked up, he's going to die, let 'em die in jail. . . .

242   Angle: NED *clutches his rosary, pulls his granny glasses closer to his head.*

NED: Where's the injured man . . . ?

BYSTANDERS (*variously*): It's the priest, let 'em through.

NED *bends over the stricken form on the floor.*

243   Close-up: as he whispers in the ear of the fallen man.

NED (*sotto*): Jimmy, I'm so sorry . . . Jimmy . . . I *told* you we were gonna get outta here. . . .

The man turns his head. It is not Jimmy.

BOB: What is he *sayin'* . . . what is he sayin' to me . . . ? Father.
I ain't gonna die . . . get 'em *away* from me. . . .

NED (*sotto; surprised*): Bobby!

WARDEN (*offscreen*): Okay, okay, the man's on his last legs.
He's ravi . . . okay. Stretcher-bearers! Get in here. . . .
Doc . . . ?

DOCTOR (*offscreen*): Move aside, lemme get to 'em. . . .

BOB: Get that damn priest *out* of here. . . .

He pushes at the priest (NED) *with his bloody hands.*

244   Angle: The crowd over the fallen man.

DEPUTY #1: *Give* way . . . give 'em room, make way here.

NED *gets up from the group. He moves gingerly, as he cannot see
because of the blood on his glasses. CAMERA MOVES with him.
He stops, looks down. He takes off his bloody glasses to see better.*

DOCTOR (*offscreen*): All right, gently, men, gently, y'have
someone run ahead and fetch my bag over to the jail. . . .

BOB (*offscreen*): I'm not gonna die, damn the lot of you . . .
I'm not gonna die here. . . .

NED *takes a bandanna out of his pocket, starts cleaning the blood
off his glasses.*

WARDEN (*offscreen*): He gives you any sass, you let him drown
in his own blood. He just killed my two best men over't the
prison . . . clear the door. You hear me. *Clear* the door . . .
stand aside.

NED *rubs his eyes. He sighs. He is jostled and turns around. A foot from his face . . .* BOBBY, *the convict on the stretcher, looks right at him.* BOBBY *recognizes him.*

BOB (*astonished, softly*): Ned!

The Procession with the stretcher starts to move through the door. NED *watches, puts on his glasses.*

BOB: Gimme the priest, I'm caught up, I'm *going,* I feel myself going. . . .

The procession with the stretcher moves out through the door.

BOB (*looking back toward Ned*): The priest. Is there a *Christian* among you . . . ?

245   *Angle:* NED's *arm is taken by the* SHERIFF, *going out of the door.*

246   *Interior: Jail Cell—Day.*

      BOBBY, *swaddled in bandages. The* DOCTOR *gets up from him. A* GUARD *lets the* DOCTOR *out of the cell.*

247   *Angle: The far corner of the cell,* NED *holding his Bible. Beat.*

248   *Angle:* NED *and* BOBBY. BOBBY *waits until he hears the* SOUND *of the doctor and the guard receding, then looks at* NED. NED *pulls his chair over by* BOBBY *and sits at his head.*

BOB: Bless me, Father, for I have sinned.

NED (*leaning in; sotto*): We thought you were dead, Bobby. . . .

Bob: It's been a long time since my last confession.

Ned: Why'd you have to shoot that man . . . ?

Bob: Whaddaya, nuts, Ned? What are you, you're a doctor, then you're a priest. Now . . . (*He coughs.*) Very good. Very good, Neddy. How do we get out of here . . . ?

Ned: Why'd you have to shoot that deputy, Bob . . . ?

Bob: Cut the comedy, you would've done it, too. I'm not gonna ask you how you got the priest togs, that's fine. Just tell me how we get out of here.

Ned: Uh-huh. (*Getting up.*) I'm sorry for you, Bob. . . .

Bob: You're what?

Ned: That you stand the gaff for the men you shot. I'm so sorry. (*Exiting.*) If there's anything I can do to make you more comfortable . . .

Bob: Neddy, you're joking with me.

Ned (*holds up his hands*): What can I *do*, Bob . . . ?

Sound Effects: The corridor door opening.

Ned *looks up.*

249   *Point of View: Through the bars. It is the* Warden. *He comes closer to the bars.*

250   *Angle:* Ned *turns his head away from the* Warden, *who comes close to the bars.*

WARDEN: Well, Bob. Doc says you'll live long enough for us to *hang* you . . . escape from prison, murder of two guards, murderous assault on an *officer* . . . (*He nods to* NED.) *Father* . . . Now you finish up, I'm coming back in here, five minutes, and I want you to tell us where the other two men are. . . .

SOUND *of the door closing behind the warden.*

251   Angle: NED *and* BOB. *Beat.*

BOB: That's *right.* . . .

BOB *looks meaningfully at* NED.

NED: What can I do, Bob, what can I do to get you out of here . . . ?

BOB: I don't know, Ned, but you better *do* it. (*Beat.*) Hey? Or I turn you over to the warden there. . . .

NED: You'd send us back inside?

BOB: Inside, hey, Ned; you know if I rat you out, we all hang for the guards we shot. . . .

NED: You shot the guards, Bob.

BOB: I think not, Ned, I think *you* shot 'em and I think that's my dying confession. (*He coughs, rises up on one elbow.*) Now, whaddaya gonna do, to help me get across that border?

Sound Effects: The door opening.

BOB *lifts his head to see the* SHERIFF *and the* WARDEN *in the door.*

SHERIFF: Father, you about done . . . ?

NED *gets up, looks out of the window.*

252   *Exterior: Town Square—Day.*

    Point of View: Outside. The Procession forming in the town square by the gazebo.

253   *Interior: Town Hall—Jail Cell—Day.*

    Angle: BOB *and* NED. NED *wipes his forehead.*

254   *Exterior: Town Square—Day.*

    JIM *is waiting for* NED. *The Procession of the Shrine forming in the background. The* TRANSLATOR *and* BISHOP *come up to him. The* YUGOSLAV PRIEST *speaks and the* TRANSLATOR *translates.*

TRANSLATOR: He says your understanding of the Manichaean heresy is populist and limited.

JIM: Uh-huh.

TRANSLATOR: He would invite you to read *his* book upon the subject, but unfortunately, it does not exist in English.

JIM: Yeah, that's tough.

FATHER LEVESQUE *comes to the head of the stairs, KNOCKS. His staff is on the ground, the assembled priests, monks, etc.* JIM *looks around. The band starts to PLAY.*

JIM (*to himself*): Oh, hell . . .

TRANSLATOR: Here we go!

JIM: Yeah.

255   *Exterior: Town Hall—Balcony—Day.*

Interior.

We hear the MUSIC from the beginning of the Procession.
NED *is seen coming out of the cellblock. In the office area of
the jail the* WARDEN, *and the* SHERIFF, *and several guards
are confabbing, their backs to* NED.

SHERIFF (*to* WARDEN): The Feast of St. Ann, they take the
Madonna, belongs jointly to us and sister parish 'crost the
river, in Canada, the *priests* walk it over there. . . .

They become aware of NED.

NED: I believe he's dying.

WARDEN: Best thing in the world for 'em. The swine just shot
a police officer.

NED: I'm going back, he's asked for another *priest* to admin-
ister the last rites. . . .

WARDEN: One down and two to go.

NED *moves out of the jail. CAMERA FOLLOWS.*

SHERIFF: Where the *hell* d'you think those other two ones
are . . . ?

WARDEN: Oh, *we'll* find 'em. Don't you worry.

256   *Exterior: Town Square—Gazebo—Day.*

The priests, forming in the square, looking up at FATHER
LEVESQUE *and the Madonna.* FATHER LEVESQUE *starts
praying in Latin, and the crowd answers. The* YUGOSLAV

PRIEST *smiles at* JIM, *who tries to mouth some Latin words as he looks around.*

257   *Angle:* NED *pushes through the crowd. CAMERA MOVES with him as he looks for* JIM. *He spots him and comes over to him.*

258   *Angle—Close-up: The two of them whisper to each other under the guise of giving the antiphonal responses.*

JIM: I couldn't get the hundred bucks. I'm . . . where the hell have you been?

NED: Bobby's in the slammer.

JIM: What?

NED: He's in the jail. He shot a cop, and they shot him.

JIM: Yeah? They got him. Yeah?

NED: Now lookit, he saw me. He knows we're here. He's going to . . .

The YOUNG MONK *goes by, carrying a large fishbowl.*

YOUNG MONK: Evening, Father . . .

JIM: Hiya.

NED: He says he's going to rat us out. We have to help him escape. (*Pause.*) We have to take him with us.

JIM: I don't get it. He said he'd rat us *out?*

NED: Yeah.

JIM: Well, well, well, let 'em *rot* in there. . . .

NED: I'm way ahead of you.

He turns JIM *around and points him toward the jail.*

259   *Interior/Exterior: Town Hall—Jail Cell Window—Day.*

    Point of View: BOB *looking at them from the jail cell window.*

NED (*offscreen*): He says either he sees us coming back to save him, or he blows the whistle, before we can get across. He's giving us five minutes.

JIM: And how do we get across . . . ?

NED: I have no idea.

260   *Angle:* FATHER LEVESQUE.

FATHER LEVESQUE: Before we begin the Procession, would anyone who has a special plea for the intercession of the Virgin, please come to my left?

261   *Angle:* NED *and* JIM *look over at* MOLLY, *who is standing, obstinate, with her* LITTLE GIRL.

262   *Point of View:* MOLLY *holding her* LITTLE GIRL *by the hand.* MOLLY *mimes "Have you got the money . . . ?"*

263   *Angle:* NED *shakes his head, slowly, no, then mimes "Please. . . ."*

264   *Angle:* MOLLY *shakes her head: "Not a chance . . ."*

265   *Angle:* NED *and* JIM.

NED: We're just going to have to walk in, try to waltz him out, dress him like a *priest,* something. . . .

FATHER LEVESQUE (*offscreen*): And now, as is traditional. At this time before our Procession, we have the traditional drawing of our lottery.

266   *Angle: The* YOUNG MONK *at the top of the stairs, bearing the fishbowl, puts it on the table next to* FATHER LEVESQUE, *who motions that he should draw the ticket.*

FATHER LEVESQUE: And I know how eagerly you, my brothers in Christ, have waited to see who shall receive this reward and this honor.

The YOUNG MONK *reaches in and draws a ticket. He hands it to* FATHER LEVESQUE, *who reads it.*

FATHER LEVESQUE: And I, oh, I call up here to stand beside me, Father *Brown!*

267   *Angle:* NED *and* JIM *push through the crowd, toward the jail.* JIM *turns back.*

FATHER LEVESQUE: Father Brown . . . Father Brown . . . ?

NED *tries to pull* JIM *after him. The* OLD WOMAN, *who is standing near them in the crowd, shouts.*

OLD WOMAN: Here he is. Here he is. Father Brown!

The crowd starts pushing FATHER BROWN *toward the front of the steps.* NED *is separated from* JIM, *looks back at him.* JIM *is borne back through the crowd, helpless.* NED *is alone. He looks up at the jail window.*

268   *Point of View:* BOB *looking down at him.*

269   *Angle:* NED *looks down, then looks around for* JIM.

270   Angle: JIM *mounts the steps, stands beside* FATHER LE-
VESQUE.

FATHER LEVESQUE: . . . as there is so much interest, and not
sufficient time, we, many years ago, latched on the expe-
dient of letting this honor be awarded by the machinery of
chance. . . .

The YOUNG MONK *catches* JIM'*s eye, winks.*

FATHER LEVESQUE: But we are very gratified it should fall
tonight on the shoulders of a great and a good man, a *pious*
man, one whom we are honored to have with us at this
enclave.

Beat.

JIM: I, uh, I never *won* anything before. . . . (*Beat.*) I'm, I'm
really anxious to get back *down* there, and let the, you know,
the Procession . . . go, so . . . uh, you *give* it to me 'n' be
assured, you have my complete . . . uh . . .

The YOUNG MONK *leans over to him.*

YOUNG MONK (*sotto*): The "lottery," Father Brown . . . (*Beat.*)
You've written of it *yourself* . . . in your *book.* . . .

JIM (*sotto*): I know I have, but that was so *long* ago.

FATHER LEVESQUE: And it is with great happiness that I
present to you Father Brown, whom, we may say, the hand of
God itself has chosen to deliver this year's sermon on the
Miraculous Properties of the Shrine of St. Ann.

JIM *is stunned.*

271   Angle: NED *points at his wrist. Looks around, disappears
into the jail.*

272   *Angle:* JIM *watches him, helpless. The expectant townsfolk look up, waiting for* JIM *to start the sermon.* FATHER LE-VESQUE *and the group at the top of the stairs move back respectfully, to let* JIM *begin. Beat.* JIM *looks around, wipes his brow.*

JIM: Ah, you know what . . . I think it's not inappropriate at this point to ask for God's help. . . . (*He hangs his head; to himself.*) Oh, my God . . .

273   *Interior/Exterior: Town Hall—Balcony—Day.*

The SHOPKEEPER *and* WARDEN *have joined the group. As* NED *enters:*

SHOPKEEPER: I, uh, I'm told that there was some *reward* associated with the capture of the . . .

NED *brushes past him and the* WARDEN.

WARDEN: We met before, Father . . . ?

NED: No, I'm sure that we have not. The other priest will be in momentarily. . . .

WARDEN: You sure look familiar. . . .

NED: All priests look alike.

WARDEN: Uh-huh . . .

The SHERIFF, *who is looking out at the Procession, shushes them. The* WARDEN *and the* SHOPKEEPER *look out.*

NED: I'll just wait for the second priest.

The SHERIFF *nods back over his shoulder.* NED *goes to the wall, eyes the keys, and tries to take them off the wall. The* SHERIFF, *hearing the keys jingle, turns back.* NED *waves "It's okay" to the* SHERIFF, *goes into the cellblock. The* SHERIFF *waves back, turns back.*

274   *Point of View:* JIM *on top of the steps across the street.* JIM *looks to* FATHER LEVESQUE, *who nods him to go on.* JIM *sighs, rubs his hands over his lapels, feels something, takes it out. He looks down at it.*

275   *Insert: It is the Colt pamphlet which he took from the hardware store.*

276   *Angle:* JIM *looks down at the pamphlet.*

277   *Insert: The pages opening. A chapter entitled "An Encounter with a Bear," the drawing of a Colt and the text below, which reads "Have you ever felt completely alone . . . ?"*

278   *Angle:* JIM *looks up. He begins to read the pamphlet to the throng.*

JIM: Have you ever felt completely alone . . . ? Alone in a world of danger, and no one to rely on . . . ?

279   *Interior/Exterior: Town Hall—Balcony—Day.*

       The WARDEN, SHOPKEEPER, SHERIFF, *etc. leaning out of the window. The* SOUND *of the amplified sermon being carried to the group.*

280   *Interior: Town Hall Cellblock—Day.*

       BOB *arranging the pillows on his bed underneath the blanket to resemble his sleeping form.*

281   *Angle:* NED *and* BOB, *both dressed as priests, sneak out of the cellblock.* CAMERA FOLLOWS *them through the office area where the other men are still listening to the sermon.*

282   *Exterior/Interior: Town Hall—Balcony—Day.*

283   *Angle:* NED *waves "Everything's okay" to the* SHERIFF. BOB *turns his face away, and they both start out the door.*

JIM (*offscreen on loudspeaker*): "Danger on every hand, in a world *fraught* with danger. And at the brink of death, I felt in my pocket and what did I find . . . ?"

Beat.

284   *Exterior Town Square—Gazebo—Day.*

JIM: "What did I find . . . ?"

He looks down.

285   *Insert: The Colt pamphlet. It reads, "What did I find . . . ? My Colt .32 Hammerless Pocket Automatic. Blue or Special Engraved Finish, more gun for the money than . . ."*

286   *Angle:* JIM *rubs his forehead. The* YOUNG MONK *and other priests strain to hear* JIM's *next word.*

JIM: "What did I find . . . ?"

287   *Interior/Exterior: Town Hall—Balcony/Staircase—Day.*

NED *and* BOB *come down the stairs.* BOB *staggering.*

288   *Exterior: Town Square—Gazebo—Day.*

At a loss for words. He looks at the audience.

289   Angle—His Point of View: Hundreds of faces turned to him, panorama of faces, the YOUNG MONK, *who smiles encouragement.*

290   Angle: JIM.

JIM: . . . Nothing. There's nothing there, it's all in your head. They can take the money from you, they can take the position from you, I don't know, they can whip you . . . people turn their backs on you. Everything happens to everybody . . . you ain't going to find nothing in your pocket that can stave it off.

291   Angle: MOLLY *and her* LITTLE GIRL *beside her listening intently to* JIM.

292   Angle: JIM *speaking.*

JIM: Nothing can stave it off. (*Pause.*) Pain. Affliction. We say "power," power doesn't do it, 'cause you never have enough. (*Pause.*) Money, I don't know, do you know anybody has enough? Still trouble befalls us. (*Pause.*) *Everyone* has got that sadness in their heart. (*Pause.*) *Some* people are meant to be hard. *I* don't know, it seems they are, we meet them.

293   Angle: MOLLY *and the kid, listening.*

JIM (*offscreen*): Is God good? I don't know.

294   Angle: JIM *speaking.*

JIM: All I know, something *might* give you comfort . . . maybe you *deserve* it . . . it *comforts* you to believe in God, you *do* it.

295   Exterior: Town Square—Day.

NED *and* BOB, *dressed as priests, sneak out of the jailhouse,* BOB *concealing his shotgun. They sneak toward the float, past* MOLLY, *who turns to* NED.

MOLLY: All right.

NED *stops.*

NED: What?

MOLLY: I don't want your money, take the kid on the Procession, pray for her.

JIM (*offscreen*): . . . That's *your* business.

296   *Exterior: Jim on Podium.*

JIM: People have guilty, *you* know, people have guilty secrets. If that's *yours*, that you wanna go *believe* in something, then, then, then, that's not so bad.

297   *Interior/Exterior: Town Hall—Balcony—Day.*

The WARDEN, SHOPKEEPER, *etc., watch on the balcony.*

WARDEN: . . . that man looks so familiar.

SHOPKEEPER: Hey, I know what you mean, I have that same coat.

298   *Exterior: Town Square—Day.*

BOB *edges* NED *through the crowd.*

MOLLY (*to* NED): Just, you be careful, and you hold her hand.

She deposits the kid's hand in NED'S *and nods to him. Goes off.*

BOB: What is this?

NED: This is our ticket 'cross the bridge.

Beat. The two look at each other.

299   *Angle: On the top of the platform, near the Shrine, the Procession is forming up.* JIM *is being congratulated by* FATHER LEVESQUE.

FATHER LEVESQUE (*shaking* JIM'*s hand*): Well, Father, as usual, your presentation is unorthodox, but your theology is impeccable. . . .

JIM *looks out at the crowd.*

The militia, which is starting to congregate, checks identity papers and is moving toward the podium.

300   *Angle:* JIM, FATHER LEVESQUE, *and all who want to congratulate him, as he tries to extricate himself.* FATHER NOGULICH *and the* TRANSLATOR.

TRANSLATOR: Interesting sermon.

JIM: Thanks, gotta run.

CAMERA FOLLOWS him away from the stage, where he runs into NED, *who is holding the* LITTLE GIRL, *and* BOB. NED *turns him back around.*

JIM: Neddy, we got about ten seconds to get outta here.

NED *pushes him back toward the Shrine. CAMERA FOLLOWS.*

301   *Angle: Tight on* NED *and* BOB.

NED: Get inside . . . (*Of the shotgun.*) Gimme that.

BOB: There's any trouble, I'm coming out using it.

NED: . . . there's any trouble, it's too late.

BOB *coughs, holds his chest.*

BOB: You cross me and you go first.

NED *presses him inside.*

JIM: What's *he* doing here . . . ?

NED *reaches down, tight, on the cabinet below the Shrine, various clothes, etc.* NED *pushes them aside.* BOB *jams himself into the cabinet. SOUND of a fanfare.* NED *looks up.*

302   Angle: The Procession is formed; a path is cleared toward the bridge.

303   Angle: JIM *and* NED *and the Shrine.*

JIM: How'd *Bobby* get here . . . ?

NED: Shut up and pick it up, we're getting *out* of here. . . .

CAMERA FOLLOWS them as they carry the Shrine down the center of the street, the LITTLE GIRL *holding on to Ned's cassock. They pass by the* SHERIFF, *who has just come out of the office, and the* WARDEN. *The* SHERIFF *crosses himself, as do the rest of the townspeople, as the Shrine passes.* NED *and* JIM *look ahead.*

304   Their Point of View: The border. The barrier raising.

305   Angle: JIM *and* NED.

JIM: I can't believe, I can't believe this... *Thank* you, God. . . .

306   *Angle:* MOLLY *in the crowds. Crosses herself as the Procession passes. She nods to* NED. *The Procession approaches the border.* NED *sees something out of the corner of his eye, half turns.*

307   *Exterior: Town Hall—Jail—Day.*

       Point of View: The armored van pulling up. The SHERIFF *and the* WARDEN *shake hands with the driver, talk with him for a moment, and point back into the jail. The driver nods.*

308   *Angle:* NED.

NED: Oh, Christ . . .

The Procession crosses onto the bridge.

309   *Exterior: Town Square—Bridge—Day.*

       Angle: NED *and* JIM.

NED (*sotto*): Pick it up. Pick it up, Jimmy, let's get *out* of here.

JIM (*sotto*): I'm doing the best I can . . .

The Canadian end of the bridge coming closer. The Canadian Procession enters FRAME. NED *and* JIM *are all smiles.* NED *looks back over his shoulder.*

310   *Exterior: Town Hall—Jail—Day.*

       Point of View: The jail. The van parked downstairs. The SHERIFF *and the* WARDEN *still confabbing with the*

GUARD. *The* SHERIFF *points inside, the* GUARD *nods, and the* SHERIFF, WARDEN, *and the* GUARD *start into the jail.*

311   Exterior: Bridge—Day.

Angle: NED *looks back. Worried. Up ahead, the Canadian end of the bridge comes closer.* NED *and* JIM *smile. From the Canadian end of the bridge, a similar Procession of priests in regalia, starting toward the center of the bridge.* NED *looks back over his shoulder again.*

312   Exterior: Town Hall—Jail—Day.

Point of View: The jail. The van parked outside, still quiet.

313   Exterior: Bridge—Day.

Angle: The two processions in the center of the bridge. The two groups exchange ceremonials. One priest reaches in the cabinet below the Shrine, takes out a vestment for the Madonna, while chanting in Latin. NED *is still looking back at the jail. The Canadian priest adjusts the garment, a shawl, over the Madonna. And then* FATHER LEVESQUE *takes a scapular off himself and hangs it on the Madonna.*

FATHER LEVESQUE: For all those who labor and are heavy-laden . . .

He makes the sign of the cross, is about to start toward the Canadian side. NED *and* JIM *breathe a sigh of relief. They all start off, but the* LITTLE GIRL *does not move.* FATHER LEVESQUE *looks down at the* LITTLE GIRL, *who is drowsy. He reaches down and caresses her. He looks at his hand. It is covered in blood. He looks up at* NED, *and* JIM, *in wonder. He straightens up and looks at the Madonna. He parts her shawl. The CAMERA COMES IN on the Madonna. The area around the heart and that area on the shawl are covered in blood.*

FATHER LEVESQUE: My God . . .

CANADIAN PRIEST: *C'est quoi qui se passe?*

The CANADIAN PRIEST *sees the blood; he looks at the Madonna.*

FATHER LEVESQUE: Oh, my God, what's going *on* HERE . . . ?

NED: Let's just keep moving.

FATHER LEVESQUE: Do you see what's *happening* . . . ?

BOB, *bleeding heavily, comes out of the compartment, brandishing his shotgun.* NED *turns back to look toward the jail.*

314   *Point of View: The jail. The* SHERIFF, WARDEN, *etc., all agitated, come running and shouting out of the jail.*

315   *Angle: On the float.* BOBBY *touches off the shotgun.* SCREAMS, *as the crowd runs for cover.* BOBBY *grabs the* LITTLE GIRL *by the waist, holds the gun to her head.*

316   *Angle: The* WARDEN *etc. running down the bridge toward him.*

BOB: Nobody follow me. . . .

WARDEN (*yelling*): Give it up, Bob, this ain't the way. We got you; now you end it like a man.

BOBBY *cocks the trigger. The* LITTLE GIRL *tries to scream.* NED *pushes through a mass of monks, appealing.*

NED: Not the girl, Bob. . . .

JIM, *at the base of the float, grabs a large crucifix from* FATHER LEVESQUE *and swings it, whacking* BOBBY *on the head.* BOBBY *falls one way, the girl the other. The shotgun slides to the base of the statue.* JIM *leaps on the float, reaching for the shotgun.* BOBBY's *head comes out, catching him in the crotch.* JIM *falls back, dragging* BOBBY *with him.*

JIM: You nuts, Bob? You wanna kill the kid?

317   *Angle: The monks staring in amazement as* JIM, *in his priest's clothes, slugs it out with* BOBBY.

318   *Angle: The* WARDEN *and his men, running along the parapet, trying to take aim.*

319   *Angle:* JIM *head-butts* BOBBY, *who falls again by the foot of the Madonna. He grabs for the shotgun, rises with it. He is about to fire when he is torn apart by bullets.*

320   *Angle: The* WARDEN *and his men, firing. People around them diving to the ground.*

321   *Angle:* JIM, *staring in horror at what has happened to* BOBBY. *The* WARDEN *comes up behind him.*

WARDEN: Well, that's one down and two to go. Good work, Father.

He shakes JIM's *hand. He sees something over* JIM's *shoulder and takes a step backward, loses his footing.*

JIM: Yeah. God bless you, too. . . .

JIM *lets his hand go, and the* WARDEN *falls backward into the water.* NED *screams, off.* JIM *turns and sees:*

322   *Point of View: The Madonna, tottering,* BOBBY's *body at its base, falling toward:*

323   Angle: The LITTLE GIRL, *looking upward, trying to scream.*

324   Point of View: The face of the Madonna, falling, growing huge.

325   Angle: NED, *leaping on the float, sweeping the* LITTLE GIRL *in his arms, his momentum throwing him over the parapet, into the water. The Madonna falls in behind.* JIM *runs to the edge of the float, looks down.*

326   Point of View: NED, *with the* LITTLE GIRL *in the water, trying to grab hold of the Madonna. He goes under.*

327   Underwater: NED *and the* LITTLE GIRL *being pulled through the sluice gates of the dam. The Madonna floats after them, eerie, serene. . . .*

328   Angle: The bridge. JIM, *staring down at the empty waters, fights his way through the mass of people to the other side. Sees:*

329   Point of View: The other side of the dam, a gigantic mountain of water thundering down to the reservoir below.

330   Underwater: NED, *struggling for his life, holding the* LITTLE GIRL.

331   Close-up: JIM.

JIM: God. Oh, God—Ned—

332   Point of View: The wall of water. The figures of NED *and the* LITTLE GIRL *are dragged through the foam. They plunge into the fury below. The Madonna follows after, bobbing like a cork.*

333   *Angle: The foaming reservoir.* NED, *struggling in the current, going under. The Madonna floats by him. He grabs it, floats with it, pulling the* LITTLE GIRL *with him.*

334   *Angle: The* WARDEN, *falling downward, like a fat seal, crying out. He hits the reservoir, comes to the surface, and is borne away by the currents.*

335   *Angle:* JIM, *the sheriff's men, monks, etc., running downward from the bridge.*

336   *Angle: The reservoir.* NED *grabs on to a concrete piling. One arm around the* LITTLE GIRL, *one around the Madonna. The* WARDEN *floats past, in the background, flailing.*

337   *Angle:* JIM, *running down, strips off his coat, is stopped by the* SHERIFF.

SHERIFF: Get in line there, you men, get in here. . . . (*To* JIM.) It's okay, Father. . . .

Around them, men reach for NED *and the* LITTLE GIRL.

SHERIFF: Johnny! Duke—Get into the water now . . . you get 'em out . . .

338   *Angle: Farther down the reservoir, the* WARDEN, *bruised and bleeding from the head, is swept onto a small sandbank. He staggers to his feet, stares around him.*

339   *Point of View: The marshes. His guards and dogs, floundering through the water toward him.*

340   *Angle: The reservoir. The* LITTLE GIRL *and* NED *being helped out of the water, covered in blankets. The Madonna*

floating in the water beside them. NED *grabs the Madonna in his arms, tries to rise, wet and groggy.*

NED: We're going back across. Back across with the Shrine. Nothing can stop us. Our duty calls.

He staggers to his feet. MOLLY, *kneeling over her child, puts her arms around his knees, breathless with relief.*

MOLLY: Thank you, Father, thank you. You saved my little girl.

NED *tries to free himself.*

NED: Don't thank me. Thank God. Now gotta get that Shrine over. . . .

LITTLE GIRL: Ah . . . ah . . . ah . . .

341   Angle: The LITTLE GIRL *points to* NED.

MONK: Oh, my God, she's *talking.* . . .

She points to NED. NED *and* JIM *come back to her.*

LITTLE GIRL: Ah . . . heee, ah . . .

TRANSLATOR: Oh, my God, it's a miracle.

MOLLY: My baby's talking.

NED *and* JIM *come closer to her. She points at* NED.

LITTLE GIRL: He, he, he . . .

TRANSLATOR: . . . Yes? Yes . . . ?

LITTLE GIRL: . . . He . . .

The YOUNG MONK *starts praying in Latin.*

LITTLE GIRL: He's a *convict.*

341A   Angle: Beat. All look at the LITTLE GIRL. *Beat. They all look at* NED.

TRANSLATOR (*turning to the two priests*): What . . . ?

LITTLE GIRL: He . . . he . . .

She suddenly becomes completely drowsy and falls asleep. Beat. Everyone looks at her, then at NED. *Beat.*

NED (*to the* TRANSLATOR *and* YUGOSLAV PRIEST; *sotto*): Keep my secret.

Through the following, NED *speaks to the* TRANSLATOR, *who translates to the* PRIEST, *and then he translates the response to* NED.

TRANSLATOR (*sotto*): I cannot.

NED (*sotto*): Please. Do good works count for nothing?

TRANSLATOR (*sotto*): Some things cannot be hidden. The girl, the Virgin's spoken through the girl, and she revealed your shame.

NED (*sotto*): Don't betray me. I pray to you.

The TRANSLATOR *whispers to* FATHER LEVESQUE, *who crosses himself.*

342   Angle. JIM *and* NED *hang their heads.* JIM *raises his head.*

343   Point of View: The face of the Madonna.

344   Angle: JIM *prays.*

345   Angle: The group turns to address FATHER LEVESQUE. *The* SHERIFF *comes up in the rear.*

FATHER LEVESQUE: Is this true . . . ?

NED: Yes.

FATHER LEVESQUE: You're a convert?

Beat.

NED: We were both born Lutheran.

Beat. FATHER LEVESQUE *sighs. Hangs his head. Thinks.*

FATHER LEVESQUE: I forgive you.

He makes the sign of the cross over them.

FATHER LEVESQUE: We all have to live with the disappointment. Thank God. Thank God for the illuminating events of this day.

346   Exterior: Monastery—Day.

> *A sunrise over the river. The warden's ferry chugging toward the town. On the monastery steps a monk pulls the bell rope.*

347   Interior: Monastery—Day.

> NED *and* JIM *drinking coffee in the monastery kitchen. The* TRANSLATOR *and* FATHER NOGULICH *stand in a line of*

monks waiting to fill their mugs. The TRANSLATOR *turns toward* NED *and* JIM.

TRANSLATOR: Quite a show last night . . . true bread and circuses . . .

JIM (*cheerily*): Uh-huh?

TRANSLATOR: A true misapplication of the teachings of Christ.

JIM: Well, we're all entitled to that now, aren't we . . . ? You keep smiling!

348   Close-up: NED *staring out the window.*

349   Point of View: The WARDEN *and his men on the warden's boat, with ropes and hooks and dragging things.*

350   Angle: NED *rises.* JIM *rises with him.*

NED: No better time.

JIM: Something funny, I would of been just as happy to stay in here.

NED: Uh-huh . . .

JIM: Isn't that funny?

NED: Yeah, that's hysterical.

They walk out of the door. CAMERA follows them.

351   Exterior: Monastery—Day.

The YOUNG MONK, *running after.*

YOUNG MONK: We missed you at matins.

JIM: Yeah, I kinda missed it, too, but whaddaya gonna do . . . ?

YOUNG MONK: Are you coming to lauds?

JIM: Well, I think lauds have their place, but as it is, we've got to get over to Canada, you know how it is. . . .

NED (*offscreen*): Father Brown?

JIM: Like to stick around and enjoy your hospitality, so forth . . .

NED (*offscreen*): Father Brown?

YOUNG MONK: We all enjoyed your sermon last night.

JIM: That's good. I'm glad you did.

YOUNG MONK: You leaving with the others?

JIM: Yes, I think we are. You know, we have to.

YOUNG MONK: We wish you could stay. (*Beat.*) The others leave, it's fine they leave . . . due respect . . . (*Beat.*) But it's quite lovely here.

JIM: Uh-huh. (*Beat.*) And *what* do you do?

YOUNG MONK (*smiles*): What do we do? Pray. Rest. (*Beat.*) Pray. (*Beat.*) A man of your piety, a man of your eloquence . . . of course, not everyone's called to the monastic life . . . life in a cell . . .

JIM: Hey, don't put it down, if that's what you do and if you choose to *do* it. . . .

NED *beckons* JIM *again.*

JIM: Well, we got to be going.

JIM *walks over to* NED, *and outside.*

352   Exterior: Monastery/Blacksmith Shop—Day.

JIM: It's funny, right? Could have stayed *in* there.

NED: Yeah, I told you it was funny, now calm down, we get to the border, you make the sign of the *cross* and over we go. . . .

They nod in agreement. They square up their shoulders, continue walking. They pass FATHER LEVESQUE, *driving tractor.*

FATHER LEVESQUE: We'll see you at vespers.

JIM: Bet your life!

They pass one of the wanted posters. JIM *merrily tears it down.* NED *looks to the side.*

353   Exterior: Shantytown—Day.

   Point of View: Molly's room empty.

354   Exterior: Town Square—Day.

   Angle: NED *sighs, faces front again.* NED *and* JIM *start walking up to the guard station. They pass the* DEPUTY *and the* OLD WOMAN. *The* DEPUTY *is carrying the* OLD WOMAN's *deer.*

OLD WOMAN: Well, I heard you worked a miracle last night.

JIM: We didn't work it.

OLD WOMAN: Oh, you didn't work it, then who did ... ? "God," I suppose?

JIM (*shrugs*): Who has a better right?

The DEPUTY *beams at* NED.

DEPUTY: Father.

NED: Officer.

DEPUTY: I think last night was a sign.

NED: Uh-huh.

DEPUTY: 'N' I'm going to make an effort to be true to my wife.

NED: Uh-huh.

DEPUTY: If at *all* possible.

NED: Go with God. Going to take a little *stroll* across the border here.

He waves to the DEPUTY. *Moves on. Beat.*

NED (*to* JIM): Wonder how that *kid* is. . . .

JIM: Long as she keeps sleeping s'll okay with me. . . .

They continue walking toward the border. In front of the border the GUARD *waves them on, raises the barrier.* NED *and* JIM *arrive at the border. They turn to look back at the town.*

355 *Exterior: Shantytown—Pier—Day.*

Point of View: The warden's ferry pulling in to land by the shantytown, the WARDEN *and his men leaping to land.*

356   *Angle:* NED *and* JIM *are waved on by the* BORDER GUARD.

BORDER GUARD: Morning, Father, Father . . .

They start to pass over.

WARDEN (*offscreen*): Stop those two priests . . . !

NED *and* JIM *turn back.*

357   *Point of View: The* WARDEN *shuffling toward them with difficulty, his head bandaged from the dam fracas, assisting himself with a walker.*

358   *Angle:* NED *and* JIM *at the border. They hang their heads. The* SHERIFF *runs ahead of the* WARDEN *toward them.*

SHERIFF: I'm afraid you two will have to come with me. . . .

They nod. They start back toward the jail.

JIM: Who would have thought that it would end this way . . . ?

NED: Yeah? Well I guess I could have predicted it. . . .

SHERIFF: Could you . . . ?

They round a corner to the police van, where a newsreel camera is setting up. JIM *is bereft;* NED *puts his arm around* JIM. *As they come to the van, the van doors are opened.* NED *looks at* JIM. JIM *backs away, looks up at the sky. He fingers his rosary beads.*

359   *Point of View: The sky. Fingers of light coming through the clouds.*

360   *Angle:* NED *and* JIM.

NED: Let's just get it over with.

They start to mount up the stairs to the van.

SHERIFF: That won't be necessary.

He restrains them, motions two men into the van. The two men lower two bodies on boards over the back of the van. The two dead bodies have priests' clothes on and wear cowboy hats.

SHERIFF: Found 'em at the bottom of the gorge. Their car must of gone off the road, the big snowstorm.

Beat. The dogs have come over and start HOWLING. NED *and* JIM *stand silent.*

SHERIFF: Well . . . ?

WARDEN: You don't even have to ask. My dogs know 'em. . . .

Beat. NED *steps up.*

NED: Yep. Those are the guys who stole our clothes.

The SHERIFF *and the* WARDEN *nod.*

WARDEN: All I want to hear.

The body of BOB *is taken out of the jailhouse and loaded into the van. The newsreel cameraman starts filming.*

WARDEN: That's three for three. Never lost one yet!

He turns toward the newsreel camera.

WARDEN: There is no escape from fate, gentlemen. As it is written, so shall it be done. Thus men pursue a life of crime. They sought death and shame, and they have received it. We have given it to them, haven't we? Haven't we, lads!

He shakes hands with the SHERIFF, *poses with him for the camera. The dogs are howling piteously. The* WARDEN *swipes at them with his riding crop.*

WARDEN (*to the dogs*): Shut up, there. . . .

The WARDEN *salutes the two priests, starts toward the front of the prison van.*

SHERIFF: Guess you'll be wanting your identification back.

He hands the documents to them.

361   *Insert: The two identity cards for* FATHER BROWN *and* FATHER RILEY, *dressed in their cowboy hats.*

362   *Angle:* NED *and* JIM *put the cards in their pockets.*

363   *Angle: The front of the van. The* WARDEN *looks back toward the two priests.*

WARDEN: Damn if those two men don't look familiar.

FATHER LEVESQUE: Are you a Catholic?

WARDEN: No.

FATHER LEVESQUE: A Lutheran?

WARDEN: Yes.

FATHER LEVESQUE *shrugs as if to say, "Well, that explains it. . . ."*
The prison van starts to drive off.

364   Angle: NED *and* JIM *look after the van.*

365   Point of View: The back of the van. The dogs strain toward
them, still HOWLING.

366   Angle: NED *and* JIM *look at each other, look at the border.*

367   Point of View: The barricades are being dismantled.

368   Angle: NED *and* JIM *look at each other, look at their identity*
cards.

MOLLY (*offscreen*): I suppose I should *thank* you. . . .

They turn. MOLLY, *carrying her sleeping child, has come up to*
them. They all start to move across the bridge.

NED: Happy to serve.

MOLLY: I suppose it's a "miracle."

NED (*shrugs*): She still sleeping?

MOLLY: Yes, Doc says she should sleep till noon.

NED: Thank God. What was she *shouting* at us last night?

MOLLY: Speaking in tongues. You worked a miracle, is that
the truth?

NED: Hey, believe what you *wanna* believe, what are you, picking a *fight?*

MOLLY: No. *No,* I'm not "picking a fight," *no.* Matter of fact, *"No."* I was "moved," I was "moved," I was "moved," I was thankful what *happened,* is that so *strange* . . . ?

NED: Not strange at *all* . . .

JIM *turns around.*

369   *Point of View: The* YOUNG MONK *looking after them. He reaches behind to his collar, shows the clothespin.*

370   *Angle:* JIM *looks back at the* MONK, *slowing down. The group continues walking.*

MOLLY: Yeah, well, then what about *this?* It *moved* me, I'm thinking about, I'll take holy orders.

NED: Holy orders.

MOLLY: Yeah.

NED: You're sure that's what you want to do . . . ?

MOLLY: Can you think of a better idea . . . ?

NED: A better idea . . . Yeah. Maybe I can . . . maybe I can.

JIM *starts to lag behind.* NED *looks back at* JIM.

371   *Point of View:* JIM *waves good-bye.*

372   *Angle:* NED *looks quizzically at* JIM. JIM *waves toward him. Beat.* NED *waves back, starts back over the bridge toward Canada.* JIM *retreats toward the American side.*

373   *Angle:* MOLLY *and* NED *walk together. CAMERA moves with them.*

MOLLY: A *better* idea ... well, you wanna *share* it with me, Father ... ?

NED: All in good time, all in good time.

374   *Angle on the American Side:* JIM *walks up to the* YOUNG MONK; *they walk together back to the monastery.* JIM *picks a clothespin off a clothesline and clips it to his coat. CAMERA follows him up the steps of the monastery. He turns back.*

375   *Exterior: The Canadian Side.*

    MOLLY *and* NED, *walking,* MOLLY *holding the child.*

MOLLY: You gonna share your idea with me, Father?

NED: Not Father. Ned.

MOLLY: Father Ned? You gonna—

NED: Just Ned.

MOLLY: You mean you're not—

He leans toward her, touches her face.

NED: I'm Ned.

She registers great surprise. The child begins to wake in her arms. NED *looks from her face toward the monastery.*

376   *Point of View:* JIM *by the water, the monastery behind him.* JIM *shrugs.*

377   *Angle:* NED *with* MOLLY. *He shrugs. He gestures before him as if to say, "Do you want to come with me?" Beat. She takes*

his arm, and the two with the LITTLE GIRL *walk farther into Canada.*

378   *Interior/Exterior: Monastery—Chapel.*

JIM *and the* YOUNG MONK. JIM *turns into the monastery; the* YOUNG MONK *precedes him. They pass by the Shrine; CAMERA MOVES with them. As they pass,* JIM *looks up at the Shrine.*

379   *Point of View: The Madonna, a tear on her cheek.*

380   *Angle:* JIM *looks at the Madonna, then at the hole in the roof, dripping water on the Shrine.*

381   *Close-up: The face of the Madonna with the tear falling.*

382   *Angle:* JIM *looks at the Madonna.*

JIM (*to himself*): They oughta get that thing fixed.

JIM *moves deeper into the monastery. Two monks close the huge doors to the outside.*

FADE OUT.

THE END